How To Become A

MILLIONAIRE

HOW TO BECOME A
MILLIONAIRE

A STRAIGHTFORWARD APPROACH TO ACCUMULATING PERSONAL WEALTH

Mark L. Alch, Ph.D.

LONGSTREET
Atlanta, Georgia

Published by
LONGSTREET, INC.
A subsidiary of Cox Newspapers
A subsidiary of Cox Enterprises, Inc.
2140 Newmarket Parkway
Suite 122
Marietta, GA 30067

Printed in the United States of America

1st printing 1999

Library of Congress Catalog Card Number: 99-65086

ISBN: 1-56352-606-9

Jacket and book design by Burtch Bennett Hunter

Visit Longstreet on the World Wide Web
www.lspress.com

For my loving wife and partner, Sharlene Rivi Alch,
and for Matthew and Nikkie—
my dear children who are part of the echo-boomers
and members of the next generation of wealth creators

ACKNOWLEDGMENTS

This book has been an exciting adventure, a lot of fun, and a labor of love. As is true in most writing projects, a number of people contributed to the final product and their assistance was invaluable. Jim Kuykendall, a trusted and close friend, kept me on track, presented many helpful suggestions, offered his points of view, painstakingly edited the first draft, and assisted in the final manuscript formatting. I also want to thank Dana Sherman, Esq., my attorney, personal financial advisor, and close friend for more than a quarter of a century, and Dr. Rick Seabold, also a close friend of mine for many years, for reading a later draft of the book. Their suggestions and comments were of great help. A word must be said for my good friend Tom Brekka, whose bimonthly chats over breakfast on various topics covered in this book helped provide direction and gave me a vantage point on how they should be treated. Special thanks go to Gayle Chanen Rapaport, an author in her own right, who offered suggestions and encouragement through manuscript rewrites. Chuck Perry, the president and editor at Longstreet Press, provided encouragement and support throughout the project. His editorial comments from the draft stage to subsequent revisions were insightful and significant. In addition, I want to thank Tysie Whitman and David Black for their extraordinary work in tightening the manuscript.

I would like to pay my grateful respects to the memory of my greatest teacher, Dr. Jere King, who was a professor of history at UCLA thirty years ago when I was a graduate student. Whatever is good in my work owes something to him, and I was especially conscious of his eye over my shoulder when I began my book. I also offer my respects to another dedicated and scholarly teacher of whom I was very fond, Dr. Bernard Brodie, formerly professor of political science at UCLA. Dr. King passed away this year and Dr. Brodie died some time ago.

I also owe a debt of gratitude to all my friends, acquaintances, and members of my family who sustained me. Last but not least, my wife Sharlene Rivi Alch, a professional in the nonprofit sector, deserves special commendation for supporting me in this endeavor and assisting in the creation and maintenance of our own high-net-worth household. Of course, the opinions and views expressed in the book are ultimately my own and none of the above-mentioned people has responsibility for any of its shortcomings.

ABOUT THE AUTHOR

Mark L. Alch, Ph.D., is fifty-four years old and currently teaches in the Business Extension Program at the University of California at Irvine, where his course is the prerequisite foundation class in the organizational change and development curricula. Dr. Alch is also the president of Mark Alch & Associates, where his mission is to help people understand how to take control of their finances and their lives. Alch earned a Ph.D. in history at UCLA and taught at the University of Minnesota, UCLA, and Occidental College before he went into career and life planning.

Alch's primary interest has been in organizational and individual change. For fifteen years, he served as senior vice president and managing director for Drake Beam Morin (DBM), Inc., a New York City–based worldwide management consulting firm. In his capacity as senior vice president at DBM, Alch has given seminars at many of the Fortune 500 companies to leading managers and executives concerned with the management of their own personal finances and careers. In addition, Alch has conducted thousands of hours of personal counseling with many of the same managers and senior executives. Alch brings a deep understanding for and experience in accumulating wealth. In his personal finances, he has used the same principles laid down in this book to become a millionaire.

Alch resides in Irvine, California, with his wife Sharlene and their two children, Matt and Nikkie.

CONTENTS

FOREWORD

I deliberated on writing a book about the wealthy for several years. My idea was to explore the nature of their lives: how they spent, accumulated, and preserved their wealth. I would look not only at the people who earned a lot of money, those making $100,000 or more income per year—to be sure, a small proportion of the working population—but also at those with more modest resources who were able to build a net worth of at least $1 million.

I felt there were important lessons in understanding those who were successful at amassing money and those who were not. For example, why don't more people earning $100,000 or more per year have much to show for their efforts? How did the lifestyle choices, priorities, and demonstrated behaviors of these high income–low net worth (people with at least $100,000 in earnings but very little in savings) compare to average wage earners who became wealthy? Were there common paths average people could take that would set them on the road to riches?

Thomas J. Stanley and William D. Danko, in their seminal work *The Millionaire Next Door* (Longstreet Press, 1996), through their meticulous, scholarly research, were the first to look at America's rich. For their pioneering effort, I am deeply grateful and indebted. I was able to corroborate much of their research and take their insight and understanding in unexplored directions. *The Millionaire Next Door*, however, does not give a step-by-step approach to becoming a millionaire. This endeavor, *How to Become a Millionaire*, proposes to do just that. I will explore the developmental steps the average millionaire takes to achieve $1 million net worth. This book will look, then, at contemporary wealth creation in America: the expectations millionaires have; how wealth can be built up by easy-to-follow steps; how being frugal is still a virtue for the wealthy; how the high net worth ($1 million in net worth) operate as consumers; how to select financial advisors; how the wealthy spend their free time; how they become leaders and serve their communities; how they handle inheritance; and when and how they retire.

The major research for this work came from fifteen years of financial planning and career assistance for high-income senior executives and middle-income, mid-level managers at a premier worldwide management-consulting firm. All the names in the case studies contained in this book are pseudonyms to protect the anonymity of the clients. In addition, field interviews were conducted with people of high net worth to confirm the information.

For the benefit of the average American household,

the keys to wealth creation will be explained in this book. It will probably not come as a surprise that high-net-worth families operate differently from other economic groups. Inherently, money does not define happiness, and there is a considerable amount of research that shows that wealthy individuals are not, by and large, more content. Too often, wealth disconnects people, gets in their way, and keeps them from having a productive life and being happy. Wealth, however, does help facilitate life choices and opportunities.

The lessons learned from the high net worth apply to any family in all economic walks of life. If your desire is to become more prosperous, no one will be able to hold you back once you understand what is involved. There are families with a gross annual income of $20,000 that can become quite well-to-do, although the average family's gross annual income necessary to create a net worth of at least $1 million is closer to $40,000, in today's dollars.

1

LIMITLESS OPPORTUNITY

CAN YOU BE A MILLIONAIRE? YES, YOU CAN. DO you have to win the lottery? Do you have to wait until a rich relative dies and leaves you $1 million in his will? Do you have to find a priceless antique, dusty and forgotten in the attic? Do you have to be able to throw a hundred-mile-per-hour fastball? Do you have to become an entrepreneur and take an Internet company public?

No, you don't have to do any of those things to become a millionaire. Most millionaires don't. Most millionaires are people not unlike you. Many of them are entrepreneurs or work for themselves, but just as many others have regular jobs like you do.

Your job doesn't even have to pay you a lot of money. If you have a job, all you have to do is keep it. If you want to become a millionaire, you must remember this: it isn't how much money you make, it's how much money you keep.

By the time you finish this book, you will know that becoming a millionaire isn't very complicated. It also isn't easy. It takes discipline and self-control and it may take your entire working life. But you don't have to be a genius. You just have to know that you want to be a millionaire and be willing to pay the price.

As the following chapters will show, millionaires are different. They follow their own path. Very few people become millionaires by luck or without planning well in advance. They work toward becoming millionaires every day of their lives. They also visualize that they have already become millionaires and make life decisions accordingly.

Let's understand what this book is about and what it isn't. It isn't about becoming super-rich. If you want to be Bill Gates, you will have to go out and build a company as big and successful as Microsoft. It isn't about being as wealthy and glamorous as the television families on *Dallas* or *Dynasty*.

This book is about accumulating a net worth of $1 million by the time you retire. If you can do that, you should be able to enjoy your retirement without anxiety.

Maybe you think $1 million isn't very much. To be sure, $1 million today does not remotely resemble what having $1 million meant a hundred years ago. At the turn of the century, prior to the advent of the federal income tax, $1 million was a princely sum. Even at the close of the World War II, $1 million represented a fortune. After all, the average car sold for about $700 and the average pay for a production worker was only about $2,000 a year.

After World War II, business executives and physicians who earned $10,000 per year were considered well-to-do. In 1999, the average executive in a mid-sized organization earned in the neighborhood of $150,000 in salary and bonus. So $1 million fifty years ago would probably be worth $15 million to $20 million today.

Yet, only 4.1 million out of 100 million American households in 1999 can boast of $1 million in net worth, up from a 1996 statistic of 3.5 million reported in *The Millionaire Next Door*. If you can retire with that much money, you can be financially independent. If that $1 million is earning 10 percent a year, you can live out your retirement on $8,333 a month. For a lot of ordinary working couples, that might be more money than they earned during their best years at their job.

How these 4.1 million families got to $1 million is an interesting story, but one that hasn't been written about very much. The media is generally far more interested in small subgroups like the super-rich—such as Bill Gates or Sam Walton, who founded Wal-Mart—or celebrities who make a lot of money, like movie stars, athletes, television personalities. The media focus on these two groups distorts our image of how most millionaires actually live.

The super-rich are capable, of course, of living any way they desire. But the second group can be labeled the high income–low net worth. Very few celebrities have long careers—athletes in particular have a limited number of peak earning years—and unfortunately few of them invest their money wisely. Instead, they often lead a lifestyle that apes the super-rich and costs them most of what they make every year. Then the big paychecks stop coming and they have little or nothing to fall back on.

As we will see, too many Americans are seduced by the example of the high income–low net worth. Your objective should be to do the opposite. Pay attention to the characteristics of high-net-worth families and let them be your guide. Understand that while some high-income earners retire with significant net worth in spite of their profligate lifestyles, many of them do not. And understand that many people with average incomes accumulate greater net worth than high earners.

One of the newest examples of families who earn very little yet quickly accumulate wealth are the immigrant families from southeast Asia. By pooling their family resources—money, labor, energy—and opening small businesses they produce wealth in a short period of time.

You may not believe this, but middle-income families ($40,000 in yearly income) have a better chance of accumulating a net worth of $1 million than families that make more than $100,000 a year. Why? Because they are less likely to be seduced by the example of the high income–low net worth.

The good news is that there are more opportunities to become a millionaire today than ever before. This is a golden age of wealth creation for families of average income. The investments everyone has access to—real estate and the stock market—are booming. The stock market has been rising almost unchecked since the early 1980s. Real estate has suffered through some slack periods in the last thirty years, but the baby-boom generation of two-income families has pushed home prices significantly higher over time.

Our economic future may hold more of the same. Inflation appears to be under control. Industries that didn't exist a decade ago are driving the economy. So many new jobs are being created that unemployment is at a level not seen before in our lifetime. Most of those new jobs are being created by small companies sparked by a boom in entrepreneurship.

Successful entrepreneurs make up a significant percentage of the 4.1 million high-net-worth households. People who work for large companies are making fortunes, particularly if they are important enough to receive stock options as part of their compensation packages. But even ordinary wage earners can produce a high net worth if they plan ahead and exercise self-discipline. In some cases, they have a greater shot at high net worth because they have more time to spend managing their financial portfolios and don't need to impress clients or colleagues with a fancy lifestyle.

One of the key characteristics of millionaires of any stripe is that they have a passion for what they do. Work gives them a sense of fulfillment and meaning. They plunge into their work wholeheartedly and they do not dwell on the fear of failure. If they suffer a setback or two along the way, they brush themselves off and go after their goal with an even greater resolve.

Another characteristic of the high net worth is they display the same type of urgency, intensity, and commitment with regard to their finances that they do with their livelihood. They know that as soon as you begin working towards a goal, you begin reaping benefits. Thoughts and actions are inextricably woven together.

In the following chapters we'll explore the relatively simple ways almost anyone can become a millionaire if they are willing to pay the price required. We'll also talk about how to preserve your growing assets. We'll look at how millionaires manage their lifestyles and protect their families from disasters both man-made and natural. And we'll talk about how to get the most out of retirement.

Along the way, we'll find out just how the high net worth are different and worth emulating. The high-net-worth family often is a throwback to a more traditional time and they believe in things that have been relegated to the refuse bin in our modern, post-industrial economy. Here is a preview of the thirteen common factors that set them apart from the general population.

1. They live well below what they earn.

2. By living a frugal lifestyle, the high net worth are able to invest over a long period of time.

3. They resist the temptation to spend their invested gains.

4. As consumers, they tend to be moderate and economically conservative.

5. They are interested in utility and quality in their purchases.

6. They neither show nor need to display outward manifestations of high social or economic status.

7. They have created wealth on their own and have not inherited or married into it.

8. They tend to display long-term stability in their marriage, neighborhood, and community.

9. The high net worth search out financial advisors rather than go it alone.

10. The high net worth contribute time and energy freely to community organizations. They leave money to charities, nonprofit organizations, and educational institutions.

11. As a general rule, they become leaders in community, professional, educational, nonprofit, and civic organizations.

12. As a group, the high net worth are planners and visionaries. This extends into their retirement.

13. They display an uncommon passion for their work and for saving and investing.

Whether you work in a corporation or own your own firm, whether you earn $20,000 or more than $100,000 per year, the possibility of becoming a millionaire is reachable for the average American. When you begin working toward attaining $1 million net worth, you become part of a rare breed: one of the few people in the entire country who is deliberately setting out to become wealthy and gain control of their financial destiny. Out of every one hundred people, you are in the top 5 percent.

Consider the alternative. No one really wants to be unsuccessful. No one wants a life constantly filled with worry, fear, and frustration. No one wants a mediocre life.

No one wants to enter retirement nearly broke. Instead of working for the dream of others, start working for your own dream.

Countless people are playing the state lotteries or gambling in some fashion in hopes that a lucky break will make them rich. They do not understand that you cannot receive something for nothing. Other people become the naive prey of scam artists and "Ponzi schemers," who befriend them in hopes of separating them from their money. But there really is no shortcut to building wealth, despite the colorful sales talk of these high-pressure promoters who peddle their wares like sideshow barkers. In the end, people who try to delude others only fool themselves. The only way prosperity and abundance can be increased is through the mutual exchange of goods and services. It is a fact that economic return is in direct proportion to the service rendered to others.

From time to time, you may forget parts of this book. You may want to reread passages and reacquaint yourself with certain sections. But if you are truly interested in becoming a person with a high net worth, you will take to heart the basic lessons set out here, because they are based on many years' worth of experience with America's wealthy. The priorities, choices, and lifestyles undertaken by high-net-worth households and explained in these pages can set you on your way to becoming a millionaire.

SIGNPOSTS

LIMITLESS OPPORTUNITY

What do we know about America's millionaires? How hard is it to join their ranks?

1. BECOMING A MILLIONAIRE HAS NOTHING TO DO WITH HOW MUCH MONEY YOU MAKE—IT HAS TO DO WITH HOW MUCH MONEY YOU KEEP.

a. You don't have to earn a huge salary to become a millionaire. You simply have to be disciplined enough to plan carefully for many years.

b. This book can teach you how to accumulate a net worth of $1 million by the time you retire. This amount will give you financial freedom in your later years.

c. Only 4.1 million out of 100 million American households have a net worth of $1 million or larger.

2. MOST AMERICANS ARE SEDUCED BY THE SPENDING HABITS OF THE RICH.

a. The media focus on celebrities, athletes, and the super-rich distorts the picture of how most average millionaires live.

b. The "high income–low net worth" group emulates the excessive habits of the super-rich, spending everything they earn with no thought to the future.

c. If you want to become a millionaire, you must learn to do the opposite of what the high income–low net worth group does.

3. THERE ARE MORE OPPORTUNITIES TO BECOME A MILLIONAIRE TODAY THAN EVER BEFORE.

a. The investments of real estate and the stock market are booming.

b. Inflation seems to be under control.

c. New industries in the marketplace are creating jobs at an amazing rate.

4. THE "HIGH NET WORTH"—TODAY'S MILLIONAIRES— ARE DIFFERENT FROM THE MAJORITY OF AMERICANS.

a. They are passionate about both their job and their financial planning.

b. Their spending habits and values often harken back to a simpler time.

c. They demonstrate thirteen common factors that set them apart from the general population. We will discuss those factors during the course of the book.

5. THE LESSONS IN THIS BOOK CAN TEACH YOU HOW TO BECOME A MILLIONAIRE. YOU JUST HAVE TO HAVE THE SELF-CONTROL AND THE PATIENCE TO FOLLOW THEM.

2

EVERYONE WANTS
TO BECOME WEALTHY

AS A CHILD, YOU MAY HAVE WATCHED EXPENSIVE cars drive by your neighborhood and looked at pictures of mansions in magazines. You probably wanted to know about the lives of millionaires. You probably wanted to know about their children and how wealth—being able to afford the nicest·clothes, expensive toys, their own playhouse, dream vacations—made their lives different. If you were raised in a middle-class family like millions of other children, you and your parents might not have known any millionaires personally. Since the vast majority of us did not grow up in high-net-worth households, our point of reference is the striving middle class.

Your family more than likely urged you while growing up to succeed in school, to find an occupation you would enjoy, and live an average middle-class life, the same way they did. To be pegged that way sells short our creativity and our capacity to change. Molded by society and the expectations of parents and peers, we tend to live ordinary lives and strive to afford the same material possessions our neighbors have acquired. We become one of the Joneses. Although we attempt to push ourselves a little further ahead, we really fall further behind in the attempt to become rich.

If you ask your family and friends if they want to be successful, the answer would be an unqualified yes. You could ask a total stranger on the street and you would receive the same answer. Ask them their definition of success, and they would talk about money: to afford the things they desire most. In a word, they would want to be rich. Most of them figure that rich people are successful because they have a lot of money. In reality, people have money—in this case at least $1 million in net worth—*because* they are successful, not the other way around. The formula for a larger net worth is combining a diligent savings and investment program with living well below your income level throughout your working life.

High-income workers, the 9 percent of households earning more than $100,000 annually (up from 5 percent of households with this income level in 1993), have the resources to easily join the $1 million-net-worth group. It would make sense statistically that a greater proportion of this group become millionaires. But in reality, middle-income and lower-income workers are just as likely, if not more so, to acquire wealth. They do not have pretensions about what wealth will do for them. Most middle-income and lower-income people have a strong family identification, sturdy core values, and are not bent on acquiring material possessions just so they can feel good about themselves.

For ethnic minorities particularly, the pursuit of wealth keeps them focused on the future, emphasizing the potential rewards for economic success. Unlike the upper-middle-class, high income–low net worth group, they are less interested in social recognition and luxurious living. They are used to struggle and understand life cannot exist without it.

If you continue your questioning and ask anyone on the street why they get up in the morning and go to work, the answer would astound you. The usual reply is because everyone else does it. They need to work in order to survive economically. They act in the same way as everyone else because they conform. People rarely reflect on their circumstances and what they really want in life.

Success is not measured by the size of one's wallet alone. Success could be achieving any worthwhile goal. Someone who wants to become a scholar has to put in long years of difficult study and probably will not make much money as a professor. A pastor or rabbi measures their success in terms of their religious devotion and service to their congregation. A wife who wants to stay at home to raise her kids measures her success by how her children turn out. A person who sets out, plans for, and achieves retirement with a net worth of $1 million would also be a success.

If you ask people what they would do differently if they awoke one morning with $1 million magically in the bank, most of them would probably say they would quit work, buy a dream home, purchase an expensive automobile, and take a fabulous trip. Of course if they had that much money, it would probably create tremendous discord in their lives. The average person doesn't have goals for their financial future. Instead, people tend to react emotionally to the circumstances around them.

Goals are important. They set the framework of your life. Success only happens when you work at it. It does not fall into someone's lap without effort and hard work. In the next six years it is predicted the number of millionaires will grow by 20 percent. This means by the year 2005, out of one hundred people at the normal retirement age of sixty-five, only one will be wealthy ($5 million net worth or more), four will be financially independent ($1 million to $4.9 million net worth), forty-one will still be working, and fifty-four will be broke. (See Figure 1)

FIGURE 1
RETIREMENT IN 2005

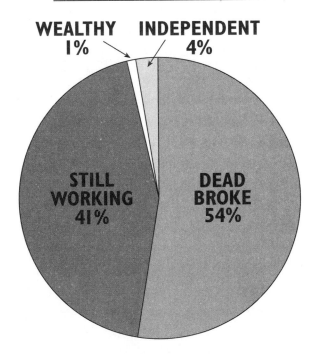

WEALTHY 1%   INDEPENDENT 4%

STILL WORKING 41%   DEAD BROKE 54%

There are practical reasons for becoming a millionaire and other reasons that raise false expectations and lead to despair.

UNREALISTIC REASONS
FOR BECOMING A MILLIONAIRE

1. I CAN PURCHASE ANYTHING I WANT.

People who spend money freely without a thought to cost will not have it for long. Look at high income–low net worth executives and managers who are downsized. Without much in the way of savings past a severance package, many executives have their spouses return to work. In many cases, they will put their house on the market and take the first job offered, even if it entails a relocation across the country.

For example, Michael R., a sales manager for a beverage company, rented his house with a prime Pacific Ocean beach address and moved to Atlanta. He would have preferred to remain in Southern California but did not have the financial resources to job-hunt for an extended period. As another example, Michelle C., a real estate executive, bought a lot and had a custom-built home constructed on it, but soon put it up for sale when she lost her job. No longer able to meet the high mortgage payments, property taxes, and insurance, she wanted to get out from under a large expense so she moved to Phoenix, Arizona, where the real estate market was booming and executive homes were far less expensive than in the Los Angeles market.

Although $1 million is a lot of money, it takes more

than $10 million to get to a level where cost isn't a concern. For those of more modest means, uncontrolled spending has gotten many a person in trouble.

The general rule is to have between three and six months' worth of savings accessible in liquid assets, such as a bank account or certificate of deposit, in case you lose your job. This may be fine for an employee with an average wage, but not for people with high incomes, entrepreneurs, or those in specialized industries who may have to switch careers or possibly spend years looking for their next opportunity. To build a sizeable estate, one has to forgo purchasing trendy, upscale items the middle class has come to view as the privilege of the rich.

2. I WILL NO LONGER HAVE TO TAKE ORDERS FROM OTHERS.

This is another fallacy of wealth creation. Everyone has a boss. Even if you are an entrepreneur, you have clients or customers who ultimately decide whether or not you will stay in business. Chief executive officers and chairpersons of large corporations are beholden to the board of directors and shareholders. Even people who attain high net worth can suffer outright hostility if their financial circumstances become known to their associates, subordinates, or bosses.

3. ONCE I AM RICH, PEOPLE WILL HAVE A DIFFERENT OPINION OF ME.

People who become rich commonly believe they can easily upgrade to a new social class. "Old Money" often does not freely interact with new arrivals. There is no big welcoming party once one reaches a certain income level—it takes a long time to build connections, trust, and friendships.

Another version of this myth is that your friends will respect and defer to you now that you are a member of the economic elite. Psychologist Abraham Maslow, a prolific writer on human motivation, once said that if he wanted to destroy someone, he could think of no better way of doing it than to suddenly give that person $1 million. Maslow believed only a wise and strong person could use that large a sum of money to their advantage. He believed the newly coined millionaire would soon lose family, friends, and eventually the money itself. For this reason, it is a wise decision not to let neighbors and coworkers learn about your financial situation.

People interested in social climbing will inevitably find others who are recent additions to the $1 million club, who will be looking for the same validation and respect.

4. I WILL BE ABLE TO MINGLE WITH THE RICH AND FAMOUS.

Though being wealthy might put you in a different circle of friends, high-net-worth couples generally associate with the same friends they grew up with, live next to, and work with. If the high net worth rarely interact socially with the Old Money, it is equally true that they rarely join the *nouveau riche* "fast crowd" who own mansions, ultra-expensive automobiles, and high-priced country club memberships. The *nouveau riche*, unlike the Old Money, are approachable—but their numbers swell and shrink as fortunes are quickly made and lost. Families that try to run in the same circles as entertainers, sports figures, and captains of industry will use up their wealth in short order.

5. I COULD RETIRE IF I HAD $1 MILLION IN THE BANK BY THE TIME I AM FORTY.

Most people have not given enough attention to what they will do when they retire. Without a detailed plan, it is very easy for someone to become disenchanted, even bored. This is a mistake often made by people leaving the workforce at the normal retirement age of sixty-five, not to mention those who attempt early retirement in their forties and fifties.

Charles L., a former president of a pharmaceutical distribution company, decided to purchase a remote parcel of land in a Connecticut bay. After taking several years to build his dream home and outfit it with custom-made furniture, Charles retired. After spending a year in his completed home, he remarked that he had regretted his decision within two months of moving there. His lifestyle was now more that of a recluse than a former head of a large company, and he had built a white elephant of a house that would be difficult to sell.

For people with possibly forty to fifty years of life left, it is crucial to have a plan, and a backup plan, for old age. The blending of education, work, and retirement gives more choices today than ever before. Many newly retired couples go on extensive travels. A common trend is to rent or borrow a motor home to visit children or grandchildren for extended periods. A hobby or dormant career interest could finally be turned into part- or full-time work.

6. I WANT TO LEAVE WEALTH TO MY CHILDREN SO THEY WILL NOT HAVE TO STRUGGLE.

Studies have shown the children of the rich and famous are less productive when given an inheritance than if they have to make their own way in the world. In high income–low net worth families, parents use money to control their children. Likewise the threat of losing an inheritance can strip away independence and self-confidence. Many parents do not realize a child's self-image can be irreparably damaged by not having the opportunity to make it on their own.

In our grandparents' time, the Great Depression was instructive to the generation growing up in and living through the 1930s, for the good life of the 1920s came to an abrupt and unexpected end. It is worth noting that the largest group of high-net-worth households are those who lived during and right after this era. While it is true the older generation had more years to accumulate wealth, the events of the period forced them to get ahead and become financially independent. No safety net existed then. Whereas those living through the 1920s and 1930s believed it was natural to wait for the next big market crash, the generation coming at the heels of World War II was raised on short-term investing and spending their gains.

7. I WILL MARRY INTO WEALTH.

This is what I call the "once upon a time . . . they lived

happily ever after" myth. For a carefree, lazy person the rationale is easy to buy into, but it is based upon a fallacy about how families operate. The problem with believing that marrying into money can bring a life of ease is that the money belongs to someone else. Lance B., a bank vice president, married a wealthy Newport Beach dowager nearly twice his age. Thinking he was embarking on a life of idleness and leisure, he was surprised when his new wife abruptly burst his bubble by insisting he continue to work and pay his own expenses. When they split up two years later, he was back at square one, thanks to a prenuptial agreement.

By the same token, Harold S., a wealthy entrepreneur who owned a dry-cleaning operation, married a newly arrived immigrant half his age after a three-month whirlwind romance, but without a prenuptial agreement. Within days of the marriage she moved back to her native country, contracted long-distance with an American divorce attorney, and sought an annulment plus a large cash settlement.

If a person marries into a high income–low net worth family, he is attaching himself to an upwardly mobile family with little discretionary income. The breadwinner more than likely works for a corporation and can't provide the new in-law a job.

Marrying upward into a wealthy family can also spell trouble another way. A wealthy family often raises their children with very high expectations of the type of lifestyle they should lead. Should the child marry a person who cannot match the family's financial success, the union is set up for failure.

A suitor cannot expect this strategy to work in a

high-net-worth family either. High-net-worth families are tight-knit organizations. Money is not squandered on unnecessary expenditures, family members are not indulged, and it is expected that every member pull their own weight if they work in the family enterprise. As long as the relationship among family members remains smooth, a family may put the outsider to work.

In one such instance, Barry T. married into a family-run real estate development company. His father-in-law was the chief executive officer and president; the eldest son, the executive vice president; Barry's wife, treasurer and an officer of the company; and Barry, a vice president but not an officer. Barry's eventual ouster from the company was caused by his continually petitioning the father-in-law to be the next in line to be president. Obviously, the eldest son was the natural successor for that leadership role. As he was still married into the family, Barry received a generous severance allowance and assistance in making contacts for a job with other real estate firms in the area.

In cases where the new family member does not work as hard as expected—meaning long hours, little vacation or time off, and utmost devotion to the firm—there is no reason to believe the business relationship will work out. The family head will very rarely put up with a lesser work ethic.

PRACTICAL REASONS
FOR BECOMING A MILLIONAIRE

I. WEALTH MEANS THE OPPORTUNITY TO FIND THE JOB YOU REALLY WANT.

The high-net-worth class prizes independence and self-sufficiency above all. They want to be the captains of their own destiny and know they can change their life's path with little interruption or interference should they so desire. Having a high net worth allows affluent business leaders and middle managers to leave the corporate world if they so desire for new careers in teaching and nonprofit organizations. The majority avers that becoming financially secure and leaving their corporate job was the best thing that could have happened to them.

In Abraham Maslow's defining work, his development of the well-known hierarchy of needs, only 4 percent of the population operate at the higher rungs of esteem and self-actualization. Maslow believed people at these highest stages of the "hierarchy" (those past the three lower stages of having their physical needs met, security, and social belonging) tended to achieve some measure of affluence and therefore tended to shape their own destinies.

Several generations ago, education preceded gainful employment, which was followed by retirement at age sixty-five. Today people can take advantage of education at just about any time in their lives. Distance learning and adult education serves the twenty-five- to forty-five-year-old worker, and several universities have established college courses over the Internet. With turbulent change occurring in the workforce, high-net-worth people are in much better control over their lives. Members of the high-net-worth class do not have to settle for the same occupation if they relish a change. They can still pay the mortgage while the transition is undertaken.

Take Hugh M., an executive in a life insurance company who had formerly worked in the aerospace industry.

Earlier in his career, Hugh worked on fail-safe devices for the Mercury space project. The strain of this job led him to switch to the insurance field. Facing another career change due to downsizing, Hugh decided on a job in interactive graphics that took advantage of his computer prowess. He enrolled in a technical institute and graduated near the top of his class. Shortly afterward, he received an offer from a major architectural and engineering corporation.

2. YOU CAN SPEND YOUR SPARE TIME IN WAYS OF YOUR OWN CHOOSING.

High-net-worth individuals find that they have more time to devote to their teenage sons and daughters. They have the time and the means to pay for any expert sports coaching or specialized arts, music, and dance instruction that their children show an interest in.

Affluent households have time and energy for professional organizations and community service, more so than the average middle-class family. They also have a propensity to take active leadership roles.

3. YOU CAN TEACH YOUR CHILDREN THE ECONOMIC REALITIES OF LIFE.

Children who are given an allowance at a young age, taught to save, and held accountable for their financial decisions are well on their way to making sound financial judgments when they become adults. Choices on how to save and when to spend are powerful learning experiences. On the other hand, children who are indulged by their parents—and who watch parents who indulge themselves—do not teach their children the value or role of money.

The typical high-net-worth family does not live much differently than the average American household. Money is treated as a scarce resource and children are normally kept in the dark about the family's finances until they are adults. Parents are careful not to give the impression that the children can receive any material possession their heart desires.

High-net-worth parents understand that wealth cannot purchase happiness. They teach compassion for people down on their luck. The message is that life is what you make it and there are no shortcuts. The typical high-net-worth family expects each family member to own up to their responsibilities and be accountable for their actions.

SIGNPOSTS

EVERYONE WANTS TO BECOME WEALTHY
Exploring the reasons why you want to be wealthy.

1. THE PUBLIC'S IMAGE OF THE WEALTHY HAS BEEN DISTORTED.

a. Most of the media focus on the ultra-wealthy—those having in excess of $10 million in net worth. These families represent only 6 percent of the millionaires (246,000 out of the 4.1 million millionaire households).

b. People have bought into popular conceptions that to be rich means they can afford anything they desire. This is a fallacy except for the ultra-wealthy.

c. The average American has been conditioned to accept their place in life: education, job, income level, lifestyle, and spending habits. Most Americans believe that only fate or luck might intercede to make them wealthy.

2. IF YOU ASK AVERAGE PEOPLE, YOU WOULD FIND NEARLY EVERYONE WANTS TO BE RICH.

a. Most people figure the rich are successful because they have a lot of money. The opposite is true—people acquire a lot of money because they are successful at saving and investing.

b. Many believe that money brings happiness. A number of studies have shown this is untrue. Instead, financial independence affords a wider array of choices and options, and a freedom from anxiety and worry.

c. High-income earners have more resources and a head start to accumulating $1 million in net worth, but middle- and lower-income workers are more likely to become millionaires.

d. Families have to define financial success for themselves and decide whether to sacrifice for the future.

3. THE FINANCIAL PROBLEMS OF THE VAST MAJORITY OF PEOPLE ARE CAUSED BY LACK OF FORESIGHT AND PLANNING.

a. Anything worthwhile in life takes planning, effort, and patience.

b. The average person has not set occupational or financial goals. Most people put more planning into an annual vacation than their economic future.

c. At the current rate of wealth creation, by the year 2005 out of one hundred workers at age sixty-five, only one will be wealthy ($5 million net worth or more), four will be financially independent ($1 million to $4.9 million net worth), forty-one will still be working, and fifty-four will be dead broke.

4. THE UNREALISTIC REASONS FOR BECOMING A MILLIONAIRE INCLUDE:

a. Being able to purchase anything you want.

b. No longer having to take orders from others.

c. Wealthy people will have a different opinion of you.

d. Being able to mingle with the rich and famous.

e. Being able to retire early.

f. Leaving wealth to your children so they will not have to struggle.

g. Marrying into wealth and enjoying a life of idleness and luxury.

5. THE VALID REASONS FOR BECOMING A MILLIONAIRE INCLUDE:

a. Wealth affords more choices in doing what you really want to do.

b. You can spend time in ways of your own choosing when you want.

c. You can teach your children the economic realities of life. For the high net worth, the raising of psychologically healthy children in wealthy families is extremely important.

3

LESSONS LEARNED:
THE THREE EASIEST WAYS
TO BECOME WEALTHY

WE LIVE IN AN AGE OF ECONOMIC BOUNTY. IT IS the best of times in living memory and the new century is going to prove the right time for the creation of new millionaire households.

In December 1998, the United States broke the record for the longest peacetime expansion in American history, more than a decade long. The nation's unemployment rate is at the lowest point it has been in thirty years, inflation is nearly nonexistent and the stock market has had a fantastic eleven-year run. Real estate has been rebounding since the recession of 1991 and new jobs are being created faster than in any time in recent history.

More jobs are being created by start-ups and businesses with fewer than fifty employees than by Fortune 1000 companies. Many people are going into new industries and business ventures rather than staying in the same career all their life. Today an average worker can expect a job change every three to five years and as many as seven or eight different careers in their lifetime.

If there was such a thing as the best time to become a millionaire, this would be it.

For generations, people had assumed that having money made people happy but that past a certain amount—which has never really been defined—there was a rule of diminishing returns. H. H. Gossen, a nineteenth-century German economist, formulated Gossen's law of satiety, which theorized that the satisfaction derived from added wealth decreases with each additional increment. Modern studies show that people at any level of wealth are no more content than those on the lower rungs of the economic ladder. In fact, wealth has a way of interfering with people's lives, reducing their human productivity, and even reducing their happiness and satisfaction with life.

Satisfaction instead comes from a person's work. People have continually remarked to career counselors that a great job is one so engrossing that they would do it just for the sheer pleasure of the work itself. It becomes doubly enjoyable to them because they are paid for what they love to do. Satisfaction also stems from doing a job or project well; having responsibility and accountability (in other words, having a say in their own work and work design); being able to innovate and create; and last , utilizing one's God-given talents to the fullest.

Millionaires strive for control over their environment. They want to assure themselves of a certain degree of independence from the turbulent world of change they see around them.

Having wealth also allows people to increase their circle of influence around them. The old adage that "money talks" can be updated to "wealth speaks loudest." Wealthy people tend to gravitate to centers of power and influence. They join groups and associations in a greater concentration than their numbers would ordinarily indicate in the general population. In general, millionaires have an assured self-confidence to try new projects, showing a zest for life and a certain contentment with their lives.

WHY FEW MILLIONAIRES?

It has been predicted that by the year 2005, millionaire households will control 59 percent of America's personal wealth. For the retired, women outlive men by an average of six years, which means most of the money acquired by baby boomers will ultimately be controlled by widows.

The number of millionaire households today, as I mentioned earlier, amounts to 4.1 percent of the population. That is, for the 100 million or so households in the nation, only 4.1 million are in the $1 million-net-worth category, where "net worth" is defined as assets minus mortgages outstanding and other debts. (See figures 2a and 2b.) Although there is a strong correlation between high income and wealth, the relationship between education and high net worth is less certain.

The old saying about "A" students working for "B" students and the "C" students owning the company might be close to the truth. Many entrepreneurs, the largest category of $1 million-net-worth families, are self-made. But

FIGURE 2a
COMPARISONS OF NUMBER OF MILLIONAIRES TO HOUSEHOLDS (1999)

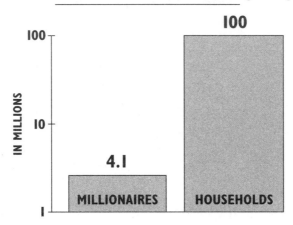

for every IBM or Microsoft, there are tens of thousands of firms that do not make their owners extremely wealthy. The average American wage earner merits around $30,000 a year, while the average entrepreneur has an income of around $75,000.

Most entrepreneurs begin their own business mainly for the independence it offers and, secondarily, for the income. An entrepreneur can eventually sell the business and make a tidy sum, but for the most part the owner prior to retirement is still deriving their living (cash flow) from the business right up until retirement.

The average millionaire, instead, makes it through long-term investing. Thomas J. Stanley and William D. Danko in their best-selling book *The Millionaire Next Door* determined that the average millionaire is fifty-seven years old with an average net worth of $3.7 million. The majority of all the millionaires in this country have

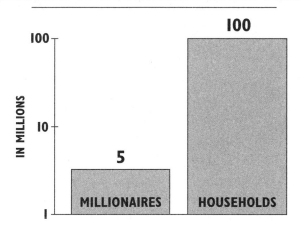

FIGURE 2b
PROJECTED COMPARISON OF NUMBER OF MILLIONAIRES TO HOUSEHOLDS IN THE YEAR 2005

less than $5 million in net worth. Only 6 percent of millionaires have a net worth of more than $10 million.

Although everyone wants to be successful, they just do not know how to go about doing it. Whether they will admit it or not, the majority of people are still looking for the quick hit. They are either not aware of what they must do to become a millionaire, or they cannot develop the inner discipline or resolve to become one.

It is not difficult to earn a living in America today. It is really a matter of how far above average you want to be. It does not take too much to become wealthy. Three things are necessary: First, produce sufficient income to fuel investment over a long period of time; second, live well below your means so you will have discretionary income to invest; third, resist the temptation to spend your invested gains.

HIGH-NET-WORTH HOUSEHOLDS

In the early 1980s, compensation personnel and executive search professionals believed if a manager or executive was earning their age—for example, a forty-year-old earning $40,000—the employee was on the fast track. This kind of emphasis on gross earnings put people on the wrong path. The belief that they needed an ever-larger paycheck to get ahead led people to change jobs frequently, each time seeking a larger compensation package. A person's earnings, after all, had nothing directly to do with wealth creation.

Symptomatic of the booming economy during this period, as people made more money, they spent more in search of an increasingly luxurious lifestyle. This carried over into the 1990s until the baby-boom generation, now in their forties and fifties, realized with twenty years or less until their retirement dinner they faced the prospect of departing their jobs broke. So the post-World War II generation, for the first time, began to address the finances needed for a comfortable, if not lavish, way of life at the end of their working days.

Although some high-income households are also high net worth, not all high-income people are millionaires.

When Exxon shut down a facility in Irvine, California in 1986, a number of people in the sales office earning between $40,000 and $60,000 a year, in their fifties and sixties, were millionaires in net worth. Each employee had bought company stock and invested fully in 401(k) plans. More importantly, they all lived well within their means. They shopped at J.C. Penney and Sears, and had lived in average, middle-class neighborhoods so long that their homes were worth a lot more than when they purchased them. They dressed in an average way, wore average watches (not gold), and drove average American four-door sedans. All were still married to their first wife.

Other professionals making more than $100,000 per year could not make the same claim. Nine percent of American workers earn more than $100,000 per year, yet not all are millionaires. Only two-thirds of the millionaire households have six-figure incomes, and most are entrepreneurs rather than employees of corporations. So the other 1.35 millionaire households make less than $100,000 per year. Although some of these people are also entrepreneurs, a fair number are company employees who simply have made a concentrated effort to become wealthy.

CORPORATE HIGH-INCOME WAGE EARNERS

The average age of these high-income individuals is forty-eight. One-third have a net worth, including equity in their homes, between $5,000 and $150,000. The middle third have a net worth between $150,000 and $450,000. The top third have a net worth between $450,000 and $1.5 million. A small handful have accumulated a net worth in the $5 million to $15 million range. This comes primarily from having lots of equity in their companies, a large salary for many years, and a habit of putting most of their discretionary income into investments.

Most high-income wage earners typically draw their identity from their jobs and spend up to their level of income.

In one instance, when Vic N., a senior manager from

an aerospace information services company, found himself without a job, he received a year's severance and immediately purchased an $80,000 S-class Mercedes Benz sedan for cash. A position did crop up within two months at more than $100,000 per year, but Vic did not like the job title. He turned down the offer. It took ten months to find another position, this time with a five-hundred-mile relocation. By then Vic's savings were nearly gone.

In another instance, Doug F., a fifty-year-old senior vice president of sales for a large corporation who earned more than $250,000 a year, received a substantial severance package when he was laid off and little else. Doug lived in a new $750,000 house in a gated development in a tony suburb near the beach. With little home equity, he and his wife drove late-model luxury cars and had about $5,000 in savings. With his earnings at a high level for years, his household could have shown a net worth close to $2.5 million, but it didn't. Fortunately for Doug, he found work right away, but in the long run he probably learned nothing from the experience.

A DOLLAR SPENT IS A DOLLAR LOST

Most people spend what they earn. When their paycheck increases because of cost-of-living adjustments, promotions, bonuses, or job changes, they spend the newfound income. Higher take-home pay means they buy larger homes, luxury cars, and a finer cut of clothes. They have not learned that when a dollar is spent it is lost forever. A dollar invested, however, can be returned manyfold through the power of compounding.

Most people believe a person is successful if they make a lot of money. But the only people who actually make money work in a United States mint. The rest of us *earn* money. People are successful because they make a product or provide a useful service that is wanted and needed by others. A measure of a businessperson's success is the ability to earn a lot of money.

We tend to believe that people who live in upscale neighborhoods drive expensive luxury automobiles. As consumers, we have been conditioned to believe successful people act this way. If they don't have the trappings of conspicuous consumption, we assume they are not successful. People in these professions, therefore, assiduously keep up the appearance of high social and economic status. They buy whatever society believes is appropriate for people of their station. Although some of these professionals and executives have a net worth of $1 million, not all do. The reality is the typical high-net-worth family lives in a moderately priced neighborhood, and they spend in a cautious and careful manner.

The high-net-worth individual has learned income spent frivolously is money wasted and gone. Small business owners, the majority of the millionaire class, realize they do not need to consume more of the "right" brands to posture an acceptable image of respectability and high social and economic status. A page has been borrowed by the high-net-worth corporate employee.

Many executives who move frequently due to corporate transfers buy a home early on in order to lock into a desirable metropolitan area—such as Boston, New York, San Francisco, Los Angeles—with a high probability that the house will go up in value. Even if the cost of housing were to rise in the future faster than their income, they would already own a home. Should they move again, they can lease the house. The company might arrange a mortgage for a home at the new location at less than the prevailing mortgage interest rate. Some companies will forgive the loan if the executive stays on for a set period. Since the idea in wealth creation is to invest as many discretionary dollars as possible and to avoid expending money unnecessarily, it is in the best interest of employees to check into these company assistance programs.

All employees earn an income from which to draw money to put into a company-sponsored or independent investment account. In addition to their incomes, many executives can look forward to a yearly bonus. This is one of the best investment tools offered to employees. Unfortunately, the vast majority treat it as income and spend it, rather than solely as dollars to be locked away in investments.

Companies frequently provide subsidies and financial assistance for their employees at all levels. The company may pay for country club and lunch and dinner club memberships for key executives. Many firms provide an expense account for client entertainment. The majority of American companies allow their employees to keep the free mileage accumulated under frequent-flier programs for their own personal use. On occasion, the company might allow the spouse (and family) to spend a weekend at a regional or national meeting at the company's expense. Employees who bring in large accounts or who win contests are rewarded with vacations or stays at a company condo in a resort community. When traveling, companies put up their executives in hotels at corporate rates and allow employees to drive to their destinations using rented cars under the corporate name.

Sales personnel and key executives often get a company car with registration fee, license, repairs, and maintenance taken care of. At the end of a year, personal miles are calculated for federal tax purposes and paid for by the employee, though this is a small fraction of what it costs to own and operate the vehicle. Employees who don't get company cars can be reimbursed for mileage when using their private automobiles for company business.

In addition, most companies encourage their employees to take college courses or enroll in certificate programs under the company's tuition reimbursement program.

THE 401(K) PLAN

One company investment program—the 401(k)—can be a bridge to wealth. In the past decade companies have changed from *defined benefit programs*, such as fixed pension plans and purchasing company stock for employees, to *defined contribution plans* where employees can choose from a variety of voluntary savings programs. The three-legged stool of fixed pensions, savings, and Social Security has been replaced by the 401(k), savings, and Social Security. Increasingly, the burden of financing retirement will rest squarely on Social Security benefits and personal investment assets. With Social Security resting in the hands of Congress, it is possible that the system could be totally altered at any time. Thus, one can only truly rely on personal savings.

The "401(k)" refers to a section of the Internal Revenue Code, added in 1978, authorizing this type of employer-sponsored savings plan. Although only a few 401(k) plans appeared in the late 1970s and early 1980s, thousands of employers soon rushed to offer what quickly became an extremely popular employee benefit. It has since become a convenient vehicle for the average employee, as well as senior executives, to acquire $1 million of net worth by the time they are ready to quit the workforce.

Today, roughly one-half of workers are covered by an employer-sponsored retirement plan. Nearly all large employers currently offer 401(k)s, and increasing numbers of smaller employers are providing them as well.

The 401(k) has three important features: 1) Pretax contributions to the plan; 2) employer-matching contributions; and 3) a wide range of investment opportunities.

The vast majority of 401(k)s permit regular pretax contributions to the plan through convenient payroll deductions. Under this type of arrangement, the 401(k) pretax contributions are deducted from the current-year pay for federal and state (with the exception of Pennsylvania) income-tax purposes. For example, if a person earns $40,000 and makes $5,000 in pretax contributions to the 401(k), the taxable salary is reduced to $35,000. If the taxpayer's federal and state income tax rate is at a combined 40 percent, the taxpayer receives an immediate income-tax savings of $2,000. The Internal Revenue Code limits pretax contributions to a 401(k) plan to an indexed dollar amount, which was $10,000 for

1998 and 1999.

Second, many 401(k) plans allow employers to match contributions made by employees. In fact, according to a survey by Buck Consultants, a New York-based benefits consulting firm, 89 percent of companies match some portion of each employee's pretax contributions. Furthermore, one out of every four companies match contributions, dollar for dollar, up to specified levels. Matching contributions are a powerful incentive for all employees at all income levels to participate in a 401(k) to the maximum extent possible.

Although roughly 86 percent of all workers eligible to contribute to a 401(k) actually do, only 55 percent of baby boomers participate. Among typical boomers, only about 33 percent contribute the maximum allowable amount. This reflects the fact that baby boomers entered the workforce when pension plans were still in vogue, and they bought into the idea that companies would take care of them in retirement. It also reveals that the majority of boomers are putting their discretionary dollars into conspicuous consumption rather than into investing.

Third, companies hire mutual fund companies to give employees the opportunity to invest 401(k) dollars according to their willingness to assume risk. Usually, the 401(k) assets can be split up among income, conservative, moderate growth, growth, or speculative mutual funds. Most high-net-worth employees place money from their 401(k)s in three to five sectors, since not all funds will appreciate at the same time or at the same rate. By the time an employee is ready to retire, a substantial amount will be available. If money is put in a 401(k) plan regularly, earns a good rate of return and compounds over a long enough time, it is possible to accrue $500,000 to $1 million net worth by this device alone (See Appendix I).

In 1999 more than 30 million workers had $1.4 trillion invested in 401(k)s. One would think all workers, and especially mid-level and senior staff, would take advantage of their company's 401(k). Surprisingly, this is not the case. A study released by KPMG Peat Marwick, one of the nation's largest accounting firms, shows a widening gap in participation rates between highly compensated and non-highly compensated employees. Their research found 90 percent of highly paid employees contribute to their 401(k) plan, compared to 64 percent of all workers with such plans. Less than half a company's new hires take immediate advantage of it. This is unfortunate. Employers are providing the opportunity for all employees to take a big step forward in their investment planning.

Some companies have boosted participation in their 401(k) plans by automatically enrolling new employees. In other words, instead of waiting for new hires to fill out and hand in 401(k) enrollment forms, the company automatically withholds a portion of their wages and directs the money to a money market fund in their name. Companies are turning to this because employees do not fully grasp how important it is to contribute—and contribute early—to a tax-deferred account.

Increased participation not only benefits the individual employees, it assists companies too. All 401(k) plans must submit to a set of annual discrimination tests to ensure highly paid workers are not benefiting disproportionately from the plan. The more that non-highly paid workers—those earning less than $80,000 per year—contribute to their plans, the more highly paid workers can contribute to theirs. Employee benefit consultants contend this helps companies recruit and retain managers, executives, and skilled workers.

Normally, 401(k) dollars are taxed only when they are withdrawn, but some people who participate in a 401(k) have withdrawn money in the form of a loan for medical or educational purposes. It is estimated that 20 percent of 401(k) participants have at least one loan outstanding. In order to continue to use the 401(k) for investment, the loan has to be repaid first. The benefit of having a 401(k) is lost unless the money is put back into the account.

Company plan administrators, professional investment advisors, and high-net-worth clients agree certain rules should be followed in setting up and maintaining a 401(k):

1. Start early
2. Be consistent
3. Maximize all contribution opportunities
4. Invest for the long-term
5. Avoid borrowing from the plan
6. Monitor the plan at least once a year

The 401(k) is an easy and convenient way to acquire $1 million net worth. Most American households have two full-time incomes. Should both partners work for companies offering a 401(k) plan and both put money away in their respective accounts, it is conceivable they will have a combined net worth of $1 million.

OTHER EMPLOYER-SPONSORED PLANS

It is also important to take advantage of any other employer-sponsored plans to the fullest extent. In addition to the 401(k), this could include an employee stock option plan. In a stock purchase plan, if an employee were to purchase two shares of the company's stock, the firm would purchase a third share for the employee's portfolio. Unless the stock drops in value by one-third or more, the employee will be ahead. In addition, many stocks pay dividends on a quarterly basis. Other companies purchase large blocks of stock each year for their senior executives up to a specified limit. Again, many people who qualify for this disregard it.

Other company plans that should be taken advantage of might include a profit-sharing plan, a money purchase plan, or a thrift or savings plan.

It is possible, then, to acquire a substantial net worth exceeding $1 million even if you are an employee of a large company, but overall the number of workers who do is surprisingly small. Some 67 percent of the high-net-worth households (2.75 million families) are made up of entrepreneurs. Another 20 percent of high-net-worth households are retired, leaving only 13 percent who work for others (533,000 households).

For the small number of employees who have a high net worth, it might be best not to broadcast that fact. It is a common myth among managers that an independently wealthy employee can become complacent. For example, some companies want their sales people to live "the good life" because it will drive them to reach and exceed sales projections.

The mergers, restructuring, and downsizing of the 1980s and 1990s have actually been a welcome occurrence for the mid-career executive who has built a high net worth. People in their late forties and fifties with a net worth of $1 million who work in organizations are too young to retire. They want to do something meaningful with their remaining work time, usually finding something else exciting and useful rather than continuing in the same field or industry, and more than likely, they will go to work in a smaller firm or company. If they lose their job, they have the financial wherewithal to find a position that fits them exactly. About 8 percent or so will go out on their own or partner with another executive to buy or start a business.

Employment counselors, as I mentioned earlier, suggest people keep from three to six months of disposable income in an accessible account in case they lose their job. People who have a net worth of $1 million can last for years, if they have to, without working. Obviously this means they have more options available should they entertain the thought of either buying or starting a business or beginning a consulting practice.

Employees who have little in the way of savings may have to choose a less-than-ideal job. They may have to accept part-time or temporary positions to keep themselves afloat while searching.

HOUSING

More people today own a home than in any other time in our nation's history. This is a reflection of a strong economy, high employment, and low interest rates.

There are three primary wealth-creating benefits to home ownership. First, property generally appreciates over time. Only once in the past fifty years—during the recession of 1990–91—has it declined.

An important consideration here is to purchase a small or average-sized home in a prime area where appreciation will be greatest. Remember the three most important terms in real estate: location, location, location.

Second, you will build equity in the house you own over the length of the mortgage and will eventually own the home outright. Then you can take full benefit of the house's built-up equity and at retirement can live in the home rent-free. This is unlike almost any other commodity that can be purchased. For example, automobiles—except in rare instances—depreciate quickly. Collectibles that might appreciate over time are too expensive and too speculative for the average person.

Third, the federal government offers a tax advantage for people who purchase a home as a primary residence. A family can deduct their mortgage interest payments and property taxes from their federal tax return. Enacted after World War II for returning servicemen, this deduction makes a home affordable for the average family. Since 1946 it has driven home-ownership to record levels.

Some home owners, though, have taken the tax advantage to an extreme. Believing that, because of the tax deductions, they can afford more house, they become "house poor" by spending nearly all of their discretionary income on a very expensive home. In 1993, the latest year in which statistics are available, only 15.3 percent of families had lived in the same house for twenty or more years. On average, according to the U.S. Census Bureau, families tend to trade up their home every 5.2 years. They would be better off, however, to buy a middle-class, average-sized house as soon as they can afford it and remain there for the duration of the mortgage rather than continually purchase larger, more expensive homes. Most people have not done the homework necessary to determine whether it is feasible to buy a high-end home and, at the same time, build a sizeable nest egg. For the vast majority of Americans it is not.

Lending institutions typically require a family to put a down payment of 10–20 percent on a house. They also figure that a home mortgage will require no more than 40–42 percent of a family's take-home pay at most. Coupled with other living expenses, this high rate will eat most of the household's discretionary income and leave little or nothing for investments.

One of the keys to accumulating wealth is to be a long-term home owner. For the average American family, a house is their single greatest expenditure and also their largest investment, since it usually appreciates in value.

Besides being an important investment tool, a home should be evaluated for its utility—after all, the family has to live there. Rents go up over time while a mortgage payment stays constant. Over the life of the loan, mortgage payments become a smaller proportion of the family income because pay progressively increases. The savings can be used for investment purposes. However, this fact is lost on the majority of the population who buy increasingly more upscale homes every few years. A costly luxury home can drain away one's ability to invest

(See Appendix II). Money put into larger down payments, home upgrades, and high monthly mortgages is not available for investment.

During the 1970s and 1980s, the value of homes grew at a pace greater than the stock market. Some investors saw this as a sure way to wealth, but this period was an anomaly. The advent of the two-income family, the first wave of baby boomers buying homes, plus spiraling inflation, drove home prices up sharply.

The recession of 1990–91 demonstrated that home prices could go down. People who bought property after the 1988–89 period saw their homes realize a negative equity in the early 1990s. That is, they were still paying off the mortgage, but if circumstances forced them to sell they could not recoup all of their down payment.

Families with $500,000 homes saw a loss of $100,000 or more, while homes worth in excess of $1 million plummeted hundreds of thousands of dollars. Not until 1997 did homes begin to appreciate again. In the summer of 1998 homes returned to their pre-recession price level. People who bought expensive homes during this time would have been much better off putting money into the sizzling stock market, which saw gains of 91 percent between 1990–97.

The average millionaire has a house worth $335,000 (up from $320,000 in 1996) and has lived in it for the past two decades. But most people cannot resist living up to, or even exceeding, their paycheck. The media and real estate agents have played up the "good life" by promoting the idea of trading up as household income increases. The encouragement can be seen in starter-home neighborhoods with few original members after the tenth year. It is, after all, in the best interest of real estate professionals to move houses.

The most recent price appreciation of homes is being fueled by gains in the stock market. An April 1999 study by the California Association of Realtors (CAR) found that 15 percent of all home buyers in the state used stock profits as a source for their down payment, up from a U.S. Census Bureau national statistic of only 4 percent a decade before. The CAR study also found that home buyers at the upper end of the market were more likely to use stock profits than other income groups. Forty-two percent of those who used stock investments for down payments were first-time buyers. There is thus a concern among experts that the housing market's greater reliance on stock market gains could mean slumping housing sales in the event of a sharp drop on Wall Street.

For the ultra-wealthy, a home worth more than $1 million is often purchased for cash. Bill Gates, the cofounder of Microsoft and one of the richest men in the world, bought a custom-built house in 1997 costing $40 million. For him, the purchase was the equivalent of an ordinary person with $50,000 in the bank buying a home for twenty-two dollars!

For the average person, though, a larger house means a bigger mortgage, higher taxes, more money spent on maintenance and services, and more money spent on decorating and furnishings—all using up scarce net-worth dollars.

Many high income–low net worth families are willing to be "house poor" in order to live in the most fashionable neighborhood they can afford. Steadily rising home prices have given baby boomers, who are entering their prime earning years, enough equity in their existing homes to make the leap to the next level if they devote nearly all of their discretionary income to home and taxes.

A common tactic used by high-net-worth households is to shorten their mortgage from thirty years to fifteen or twenty years, thus saving $100,000 or more in interest during the life of the loan. In addition to making the regular mortgage payments, they add an additional one hundred or two hundred dollars each month. This effectively reduces the total amount of money and time left on the mortgage. When the mortgage is paid off, a couple need only maintain the property and pay property taxes. If need be, they could sell their home and buy a smaller residence, move to another area of the country, or rent an apartment. In the past year the federal tax law changed regarding capital gains on residences. A married couple can now sell their home and realize as much as $500,000 ($250,000 per individual) in equity without having to pay any capital gains taxes.

SECURITY

High-net-worth households generally live in middle-class neighborhoods and do not display their wealth to the world. If they own expensive jewelry they store it in a safe deposit box and only take it out for special occasions. What they own at home is not much different than middle-class families.

If you visited their home, you could not tell if they

earned $40,000 or $100,000 or more per year. You also could not tell whether they had a net worth of $30,000 or $1 million. They are aware that outward displays of extravagance can draw thieves and other predators looking to separate them from their money.

AUTOMOBILES

The American public long ago bought into the concept of "planned obsolescence" when it comes to cars. But today's cars are more reliable than motor vehicles of yesteryear. Gasoline engines are designed to last 200,000 to 300,000 miles and diesel motors can often go between 300,000 and 500,000 miles if they are properly maintained.

Besides a house, the family automobile is the next most expensive item purchased by an American household. The struggle to project status through the car you drive goes back to the 1930s, when General Motors Chairman Alfred Sloan created a different car division to serve every economic class of buyer.

As soon as a worker could afford to, he would buy a Chevrolet. Upon marriage, the breadwinner would purchase a Pontiac. When the family came along, the household would move up to an Oldsmobile. If the family head was promoted to a shift supervisor or mid-level manager, then he could afford a Buick. The Cadillac was reserved for senior executives. This still holds true for the American consumer, although today many consumers purchase pricey European and Japanese luxury makes rather than American products. It is as true today as it was in the 1930s that as a household's level of discretionary income increases, the tendency is to purchase a more expensive vehicle.

Most American families today have more than one car and a large number of high-income families are making car payments on more than one car at a time. The benefits of a surging economy and low unemployment have spilled over into the automobile industry, which experienced its strongest first half ever in the first six months of 1999. Ford Motor Company, for example, sold more cars in June 1999 than in any month in its previous one-hundred-year history.

But as good as business is for the motor companies, the expense of buying a new automobile every five years takes its toll on the average consumer's pocket, since cars depreciate rather quickly, about 50 percent in the first three years of ownership.

The high income–low net worth enjoy celebrating their financial success by showing it to everyone. High-net-worth households know they can afford expensive automobiles but would rather watch their money increase through investments than spend it on consumables.

For many years, the interest on an automobile car loan was allowed as a deduction on the federal income tax. When this deduction ended, leasing allowed moderate-income people to drive more of a car than they could purchase outright. This gave high income–low net worth families the rationale and ability to buy a more expensive car. Taking a second mortgage on the home allowed these families to purchase an even more expensive car, while also deducting the interest from their federal income tax.

This scheme appeals to the middle income–low net worth and high income–low net worth people, who tend to spend money in advance of actually earning it.

The high-net-worth family does not concern itself with luxury automobiles just for the sake of showing off. It is not lost on high-net-worth families that automobiles sharply fall in value in the first few years of ownership. Many high-net-worth families purchase cars from a private party or dealership after the greatest amount of depreciation has taken place. Changing the oil every 3,000 miles and adhering to a normal maintenance schedule, a four-year-old car can last ten to twenty years or more. Except in rare cases, it is cheaper to hold onto an old car than to buy a new one. Contrary to popular opinion, upkeep on it will not exceed the cost of buying a new car.

A high-net-worth client, Peter W., a senior executive in an air freight company, drives a 1984 Oldsmobile Cutlass, a company car he bought from his firm with more than 160,000 miles on the odometer. Having a garage he trusts replace the timing chain and perform a valve job, he should be able to get another 100,000 to 150,000 miles out of the engine. His wife drives a 1976 Oldsmobile that is still going strong after 270,000 miles. The automobile has had the timing chain replaced twice, a valve job, and the transmission rebuilt.

The price sticker for an average American four-door sedan is in excess of $20,000. Assuming an inflation rate of 3 percent per year, and purchasing a new car every five years over a twenty-five-year span, the total expense of owning, operating, and maintaining a vehicle can cost close to $250,000. This number does not include the lost opportunity for receiving a return on the money. By not buying a new car and investing the money saved at 10 percent per year—the same rate as a new-car loan—an investor can accumulate close to $400,000.

The purchase of a luxury car makes the expense and investment potential even more dramatic. Turning in a leased luxury automobile costing approximately $60,000 every fifth year, a purchaser will put out about $400,000 over a twenty-five-year period including operating and maintenance costs. Again, if this money were placed in the stock market instead at 10 percent compound interest, an investor would add the $600,000 to their net worth plus save the $250,000 amount paid to the leasing company. (See Appendix III.)

In spite of the buying habits of the average American family, most high-net-worth households do not drive luxury imports. Millionaires in their sixties tend to drive domestic luxury cars, such as a Cadillac or Lincoln Town Car. Among the 4.1 million millionaires in America, domestic full-size sedans are the most popular purchase. Other than family four-door sedans, the pickup chosen by more millionaires in America than any other is the Ford F-150. For a sports utility vehicle, the Ford Explorer is popular. As may be expected, full-size Chevrolet and Chrysler cars also sell well.

The typical high-net-worth family purchases the vehicle outright to save the interest on a car loan. Entrepreneurial high-net-worth households, in particular, are the most price-sensitive group among the wealthy when it comes to cars. Since they are bottom-line focused, they will ask themselves whether it is worthwhile to spend the extra money on a fancy new car or to plow the profits back into their business. Because they judge their expenditures in terms of productivity and results, they usually reason it would be best to keep their high-income stream intact. They are more concerned with accruing wealth and providing additional resources for their business than seeking the approval of others.

The high income–low net worth are sensitive to what they and their neighbors drive. They purchase what is trendy and that is why so many import cars, trucks, and luxury automobiles are bought by these families. Preferring to lease rather than purchase, they are able to drive a more expensive model. They trade in their cars more frequently, too. According to the National Automobile Dealers Association, the mean age an average American family keeps a car is now 9 years, up from 8.6 years in 1996. A high-net-worth family might keep a car for a minimum of 12 years, and it is not unusual for a second or third vehicle to stay in the family for two or three decades. In comparison, a high income–low net worth household might purchase or lease a new car every two to five years.

Paying cash for an automobile and then repaying oneself is one way to accumulate $1 million. The key is to figure out the monthly payment based on the current bank lending terms. The high-net-worth household makes this monthly payment to their investments for twenty years rather than buying or leasing a new car every five years. They are making a $1 million decision whether to drive their wealth or to invest it, and they aim to have a $1 million portfolio when they retire.

Although the late 1990s is a choice time to create a large portfolio of investments, the baby-boom generation has entered the savings cycle late in the game. Financial experts agree significant wealth can still be built, but it will take a larger outlay of money each year to enter the ranks of the high net worth. Nevertheless, several things can be done immediately: 1) Invest in the 401(k) plan to the maximum and take advantage of all company-sponsored benefits; 2) remain in your current home and, as your discretionary income builds over time, put it to work in investments; and 3) keep your cars a long time instead of regularly buying new ones, and, when you are in the market, purchase previously owned vehicles at least four or five years old. The money you save should be diligently and consistently invested.

SIGNPOSTS

LESSONS LEARNED

Most people can become millionaires by taking two simple steps:

1. Begin a consistent savings and investment program; and
2. Keep your expenses well below your income level in order to have money to invest.

1. WHY ARE THERE SO FEW MILLIONAIRES?

a. There are only a total of 4.1 million millionaires, or 4.1 percent, out of 100 million American households.

b. There is a correlation between high income and wealth, although there is almost none between education and wealth.

c. Most people dream of the big, one-time hit that will make them an instant millionaire. This is unrealistic. You have just as good a chance to be hit by lightning.

2. HIGH INCOME–LOW NET WORTH HOUSEHOLDS HAVE FOCUSED ON THE WRONG THINGS.

a. Emphasis on gross earnings does a disservice to the high-wage earner. It is not what you earn that is important but what you save.

b. A booming economy leads most people to increase their spending as their income goes up.

3. **A DOLLAR SPENT IS A DOLLAR LOST FOREVER. MILLIONAIRES MAKE THEIR FORTUNES THROUGH LONG-TERM INVESTING.**

4. **THREE CIRCUMSTANCES ARE NEEDED TO BECOME A MILLIONAIRE:**

a. Sufficient income over a long period of time.

b. Living well below your means to have the discretionary income to invest.

c. Resisting the temptation to spend the invested gains.

5. **THE THREE EASIEST WAYS TO BECOME A MILLIONAIRE:**

a. Take advantage to the fullest of your company's 401(k) plan and any other company-sponsored benefits. With enough time and consistent savings, it is possible for an individual investor to accumulate $500,000 and for a couple $1 million net worth.

b. Buy a home and live in it until retirement. As your income increases, rather than buying a larger home with a huge mortgage, use the extra discretionary funds for your investments. Investing this money can bring about $1 million net worth.

c. Buy a pre-owned car and drive it for no less than twelve years; twenty to twenty-five years is optimal. Again, saving the money on a lease or loan and investing it at 10 percent interest can yield $250,000–$1 million net worth. When you consider your family might have two or three cars at one time, the savings can be staggering.

4

FINANCIAL RISK
AND SECURITY

THE HIGH-NET-WORTH HOUSEHOLD OPERATES
on a different plane than the low-net-worth family. While
the high-net-worth family lives in the present, they work
toward the future and are not distracted from their long-
term strategy of wealth creation. In contrast, the low-net-
worth family operates in the present. They are likely to
put more time in planning an upcoming vacation—setting
up an itinerary, purchasing tickets, buying travelers
checks, packing, boarding the family pet—than in planning their financial future. It is a sad fact, but for millions
of Americans there is no plan except to spend whatever
they have in their pockets. Many millions of low-net-
worth people carry a high load of consumer debt and
their financial future is bleak. They are destined to spend
their lives trying to pay off a mountain of debt. Some will
go bankrupt instead.

THE RULE OF 10

Financial planners suggest saving at least 10 percent of a worker's gross earnings. It is universally agreed this money should be taken out of every paycheck and invested. Just like food, clothing, and shelter, there should be a "payment plan" for investments. This sage advice is accepted in Japan, where nearly 18 percent of savings is the general rule. In the United States the average savings rate has been in the 3 to 5 percent range until just recently, when it dropped to less than 1 percent.

At best, high income–low net worth households might meet the average savings rate. But they are usually more concerned with living an elegant lifestyle than saving on a regular, prescribed basis. In fact, their financial security is usually limited to equity built up in their expensive home, a company 401(k) plan, and possibly a pension and company stocks. As discussed in the previous chapter, most wage earners do take enough money out of their paycheck for their 401(k) for the company to match their contribution (usually 2 or 3 percent), but they fail to contribute the maximum allowed by law. This is too bad. The money taken out of a paycheck and placed in a 401(k) is not taxed until retirement and can therefore build rapidly. The employee can also choose the kind of fund and risk he wants—from conservative, fixed rate to high growth. There may be as many as four or five gradations of risk to consider. Many high income–low net worth employees ignore this entirely and miss out on returns from a low of 5 percent to as much as 20 percent or more in a given year, depending on how well the market does. With a high interest rate and the compounding of money over time, the

401(k) is one of the soundest ways to build wealth. If people were as financially sophisticated as they think they are, they would take fuller advantage of their company's financial benefits.

High-net-worth households invest as much as they can when they get paid. They put money into their investments before any other bills are paid. In effect, they pay themselves first. They put 10 percent, at minimum, of their gross earnings into their investments. Once this becomes habit, the typical high-net-worth family increases the amount taken out to an average of 15 to 20 percent of their discretionary income by the time they are in their early thirties. By learning this simple technique, many high-net-worth families are, during their peak earning years, prodigious investors able to endow their accounts with 20 to 50 percent or more of their annual salaries.

THE POWER OF 72

While the "rule of 10" allows a household to regularly save money for investments, "the power of 72" dictates how fast and at what interest rate money can be doubled. The "power of 72" can be understood this way: if you want to double your money over a certain period and need to know what percentage of interest it will take, divide the number of years into 72. Conversely, if you know the interest rate, divide it into 72 to find the number of years until the money doubles.

For an example, if you have a savings account at 3 percent interest, it would take 24 years for the sum to double (72 divided by 3 = 24 years). A U.S. Treasury

Bond earning 6 percent per year will take 12 years before it doubles in value (72 divided by 6 = 12 years).

If the stock market returns a consistent rate of 12 percent per year, it would take 6 years for money in a stock market index fund to double (72 divided by 12 = 6 years). As a last example, should an investor need the money to double every 7 years, it would take a return of a little more than 10 percent per year to do so (72 divided by 7 years = 10.28 percent).

Considering that growth funds in a 401(k) can provide double-digit returns, it is possible to increase holdings geometrically. Compound growth gives a family a running head start to the creation of wealth. A family investing in stocks or mutual funds over a long period of time can achieve their $1 million goal by reinvesting capital gains and dividends. Keep in mind that each week or month an investor is also withholding money from their paycheck, so the investments can grow even faster than the calculations above indicate.

For executives and mid-level managers who receive a cash bonus once or twice a year, investing this money along with a regular savings plan will greatly augment the investment portfolio. This is one way for high-income professionals to accumulate a fortune in their forties, while middle-income earners can reach $1 million net worth by their fifties and sixties. It might take longer to generate high net worth with a middle income, but more people in this category have the discipline and perseverance to keep on track than in the high-income brackets, where earners are more likely to spend up to their level of income.

One of the most profound investment tools, the stock market, is an illustration of how the high net worth and low net worth behave differently.

STOCK MARKET

Since the late 1930s, the market has historically averaged a 10 percent increase each year. Performance, however, has not been consistent. Several short bull runs have produced phenomenal gains that balance out long stretches of bear markets or outright stagnation.

In April 1998, the Dow Jones Average surged past 9,000 points for the first time and became known as the "Viagra Market": an aging rally that suddenly found itself young again. After dropping 21 percent in September 1998, it quickly rebounded and established a new high (recovering nearly 2,000 points from the low point) on November 23, 1998. Although many institutional investors left the market during those two months and lost a considerable amount of money, small investors, to their credit, stood pat, and when the market recovered they showed gains. Four months later, in March 1999, the market cleared 10,000 points for the first time in history.

Crossing the 10,000 Dow barrier underscores how low inflation, modest interest rates, and growing corporate profits can make stocks the preferred investment tool for both institutions and individuals. An estimated 48 percent of American families now own stocks directly or through mutual funds, compared to 32 percent in the late 1980s. One-quarter of all U.S. household assets is now invested in the stock market compared to 10.8 percent in

1988. The value of the entire U.S. stock market has grown from $1 trillion in 1982 to $13 trillion today.

The entrepreneurial high-net-worth individual who invests in the stock market should first place the maximum allowed by law (up to $30,000) in a Keogh retirement account for small business owners. The high-net-worth individual who owns a business or is self-employed understands the risk in placing all of their money in one company or one industry; they spread their money around in the event any single industrial sector goes through a downturn, as petrochemicals did in the 1980s and aerospace in the early 1990s. To further diversify, they purchase zero-coupon bonds, industrial bonds, and utility stock.

Besides company-sponsored pension programs, high-net-worth investors frequently buy stock independently for their own account. With the advent of the Internet, buying stocks becomes easier and cheaper every year.

Nearly 95 percent of millionaires own stock and most have 20 percent or more of their wealth in publicly traded blue-chip companies. The majority of high-net-worth investors do not trade stocks in response to daily headlines in the financial markets. They do the necessary research to determine whether a particular stock will be a good fit for their portfolio.

Most millionaires agree on the following seven attributes of high-performing companies: 1) Well-managed companies have strong and enduring core values; 2) leading companies show a tolerance for experimentation. They are on the cutting edge in their industry, and are not afraid to foray into uncharted territory to try new strategies and organizational ideas; 3) they can move in new directions easily and quickly should the economy change; 4) the top managers have vision and form a strong team; 5) there is a strong sense of identity and cohesion within the organization; 6) the company makes strategic alliances with vendors, clients, and even competitors in order to win the customers' allegiance; 7) the company offers better customer service than the competition.

MUTUAL FUNDS

Mutual funds are another investment tool embraced by high-net-worth households. A mutual fund is a portfolio that may contain stocks, bonds, certificates of deposit, options, and real estate, depending on the fund's stated objective. For the investor, mutual funds offer diversification. The typical domestic mutual fund owns 139 domestic stocks, and can readily convert its holdings into cash.

In 1980 only 6 percent of U.S. households owned mutual funds. By 1998 that number had leaped to 37 percent, representing a colossal pool of capital approaching $6 trillion, almost double the funds on deposit in banks. The number of mutual funds has also expanded to more than ten thousand, and 70 percent of people investing in mutual funds have household incomes of less than $75,000. Many high-net-worth investors like mutual funds because they can look at a fund's five-year track record rather than do time-consuming research on individual companies.

The companies that sell mutual funds usually offer a large number to choose from. They are classified primarily by the amount of risk an investor is willing to assume. Although the past history of a fund is no guarantee of future expected performance, most investors anticipate returns in the same neighborhood. Should the fund not meet expectations, investors are free to switch to another fund.

INDIVIDUAL RETIREMENT ACCOUNTS

The Individual Retirement Account (IRA) was first introduced in 1974 as a self-funded retirement plan allowing employed workers without a company pension plan to contribute up to $2,000 a year while deferring taxes until retirement. The plan enables the average nonpension employee to shelter investment income and gains from taxes until age fifty-nine and a half, or upon retirement. In 1981 Congress passed legislation allowing all Americans with or without a pension to establish an IRA. For the first time, investors were able to deduct the $2,000 annual contribution from their federal income taxes. As a result, IRA contributions exploded between 1982 and 1986 to almost $40 billion.

Then in 1986 Congress passed a bill that restricted the tax deduction for married employees who earned more than $40,000 per year or single taxpayers earning $25,000. They also saw fit to restrict the IRA deduction for workers having a pension or for workers without a pension whose spouse had one instead. By 1990 contributions fell to about $10 billion, even though the law still allowed the tax deferral of investment income and gains.

Starting in 1998, a new law no longer disqualifies the employee whose spouse has a pension plan. The spouse who does not participate in a qualified retirement plan may make a maximum deductible IRA contribution—up to $2,000—provided adjusted gross income on the couple's joint tax return is $150,000 or less. The deduction is phased out when adjusted gross income is more than $150,000, and disappears entirely at $160,000.

Despite the tangled history of the IRA, it is an excellent investment vehicle. The primary benefit is that interest, dividend, and capital gains are tax deferred. It is also relatively easy to establish an IRA.

An IRA also allows a great deal of flexibility, much the same as a 401(k) or a mutual fund. An investor can choose from more than 9,000 individual stocks, mutual funds, CDs, and bonds ranging from conservative to speculative. Starting early and investing $2,000 per year in an IRA for thirty or forty years can lead to $400,000–$500,000 in tax-deferred savings through compounding. If a married couple were to use this tool individually, they could total $800,000–$1 million. Along with other investment vehicles, the IRA is an easy and painless way to help an investor reach the $1 million-net-worth goal. (See Appendix IV.)

In contrast to the high net worth, the high income–low net worth tend to put their money in liquid assets such as savings accounts, money market funds, and short-term treasury bills. These are easily accessible when the need to consume arises.

It takes time and discipline to use 401(k)s, stocks, mutual funds, IRAs, and real estate. On average, the high income–low net worth investor is not willing to take the time to plan an investment strategy. Rather than leave their money in the market for a long period of time, the wealth of information today encourages low-net-worth investors to treat their investments as a bank account. Low-net-worth investors are inclined to take profits out of the market to purchase expensive gifts, travel, make down payments on cars, and buy expensive houses.

The large profits low-net-worth investors may gain by rapidly trading stock may not look quite so spectacular come tax time. Propelled by Internet stock mania, inexpensive on-line brokerage commissions, and the overall market instability, millions of low-net-worth investors hunt for fast profits. But the gains realized on any security held for less than a year are taxed as "ordinary income." For high wage earners, the federal marginal tax rate can run as high as 39.6 percent. This means that traders with frenetic buy-sell patterns can pay out twice as much in taxes as long-term investors, who must pay a flat 20 percent maximum federal tax rate on gains realized on securities held for longer than a year. (The tax implication is worse in high-tax states such as California.)

The high-net-worth investors who do not sell their stock until retirement will face a smaller tax bite, especially since their total income will probably be lower. All in all, short-term stock traders must achieve higher returns than long-term investors to come up with the same amount of after-tax profit. A trader in the highest tax bracket would have to outperform the long-term investor by at least a 2 to 1 ratio to come out even.

Numerous trades over a short period of time can wreak havoc on an investor's record-keeping unless organization is one of their strong suits. Each trade has to be recorded on federal Schedule D, which can be a time-consuming process for a very active trader. Active traders also face the prospect of higher tax preparation fees because of the extra time and work needed. Finally, investors who reap large one-time gains may have to pay estimated taxes up to four times a year or increase their withholding on wages to both the federal and state governments if their tax total from all income sources is more than the previous year's taxes. Investors may not realize that those who fail to make these estimated payments on time can be saddled with big penalties from the Internal Revenue Service and their state's tax authorities.

Most recently, an even more frenzied model of stock trading has appeared. "Day trading" is a new form of speculation where investors hold the stock for only a few minutes before unloading it. Instead of caring about what a company produces, day traders are only concerned whether the stock price is moving up or down. Small profits can be made in an active market all day long. It is also possible to lose vast sums of money very quickly, especially on volatile issues such as Internet stocks. It is really a new kind of gambling—and you would probably be better served to try your hand in Las Vegas, since at least you know the food there is good.

Even during down markets, the high-net-worth investor does not move money in and out of the market. Plenty of high income–low net worth investors make panic-induced moves in a downturn only to regret it later. Financial experts generally advise the jittery to hold tight during volatile periods so long as their investments are in a well-diversified portfolio. High-net-worth investors know better than to change the game plan in midstream.

Just as the stock market has been an important tool for the creation of wealth, real estate, too, has played an important role in making people millionaires.

REAL ESTATE

The high net worth realize purchasing a home can play one of two roles: either a boon to the creation of wealth or an albatross inhibiting the family's ability to become rich. Using their first home as an investment, the high net worth place their discretionary dollars in rental property or raw land. There are also Real Estate Investment Trusts (REITs), a kind of mutual fund for real estate. Investors can buy shares of a REIT without actually taking possession of any property.

For REITs, replacement costs are an important barometer in estimating the return a property is likely to deliver. In general, if the price paid for a commercial property is less than the cost of building a new one, it means the buyer stands a better chance of making a profit on the rent stream generated by the building.

As in the stock market, real estate has a tendency to appreciate in brief spurts intermingled with long periods of equilibrium and a downturn thrown in now and then. The issue with both the stock market and real estate is what to do when market corrections occur. These corrections are natural occurrences in the business cycle, but the high income–low net worth take them as a signal to leave the investment. This is the wrong strategy.

While the high income–low net worth are cashing out, the high net worth are using this time to spread out their investments, so in the event one market segment weakens or declines they can take advantage of other areas that are strengthening and appreciating. They are in a position to use their extra money to purchase more property, stocks, or mutual funds.

The high income–low net worth discount or ignore the fact that each downturn in a market eventually will be followed by a rebound to levels that meet or exceed previous highs. The cycle will then repeat.

IN AN ECONOMIC DOWNTURN

The state of the economy is easy to observe with high income–low net worth families, less so with high-net-worth households. For example, in the 1980s when the building industry in southern California was booming, many executives bought expensive gold wristwatches (Rolex) and upscale motor vehicles (Porsche, Mercedes Benz, Rolls Royce). They ate at expensive restaurants where wine and champagne flowed freely.

As the industry ran into a down business cycle, most builders did not have cash reserves. A great many went out of business within three to six months, others tried selling raw land even though the prices were rapidly slipping. The few that did survive had the foresight to keep their costs low, avoid speculation, and spend wisely for material, labor, and unimproved land.

Eventually, the gold watches were sold, fashionable

restaurants watched their business plummet by one-third, and luxury automobile and boat dealers saw their business dwindle.

In good times and bad, the high-net-worth household does not change its spending pattern. They buy what is useful and needed, and always look for quality. In contrast, when the economy turns, the high income–low net worth household must cut back its spending because it does not have the same financial reserves.

The average high-net-worth household neither owns a boat nor leases a mooring at a marina. They prefer to sail on the craft owned by their high income–low net worth friend. *The Millionaire Next Door* found that the average high-net-worth person pays a mean of $250 for a new watch. Obviously, they aren't purchasing gold—and only a small number have spent more than $5,000 for a timepiece. The average cost for a new car purchased by high-net-worth households is around $25,000, a small percentage of their wealth, whereas the average American pays $21,000, representing a much larger percentage of their net worth. A majority of high-net-worth households have never spent more than $35,000 on a car, a price well within the low-end range of the luxury car market. An average high income–low net worth executive would think nothing of paying between $600 and $1,200 for a business suit, whereas the typical high-net-worth professional spends roughly $400. The average millionaire spends about $150 on a pair of shoes, way below what an average non-millionaire pays. For every one millionaire who buys a pair of shoes costing more than $300, there are at least eight people in the high income–low net worth category paying that much.

In an economic downturn, high-net-worth families are in a position to take advantage of opportunities. They do not buy just because they can get a good deal. If the construction and home furnishing industries are hurting, they might look for bargains in remodeling their home, buying new furniture, reroofing, and so on. If they invest in real estate, they might be interested in purchasing houses or apartment buildings from investors fallen on hard times.

When automobile dealerships are suffering, the high-net-worth consumer has the cash to buy a late model, pre-owned automobile—and they are not afraid to negotiate for the best terms they can. In fact, they are doing the dealership a favor by taking inventory off their hands and putting money in their cash register.

Don F., an owner of a small business consulting service, would wait until the winter months, a time when business at the auto dealerships slows down, before making his move. He would ask for bid proposals by fax from the fleet sales managers of twelve dealerships in his area. Don would give his requirements: make, model, color, trim, accessories, and options. When the quotes came back, Don would send out another letter stating which fleet managers were still in the running for his business. He would then ask for their very best offer (lowest bid), which was to include sales tax, delivery charges, and dealer preparation. After accepting the lowest bid, Don would then call the dealership to arrange for the purchase papers to be drawn up.

To reiterate, high-net-worth families stockpile their money and carefully watch their investments in good times and bad. High income–low net worth households leave the stock market as trading heads south. High income–low net worth investors typically enter an advancing market well after most of the advance has already taken place. Since they are speculative in nature, they gravitate towards speculative stocks that they have heard about around the office water cooler. Trying to guess whether a stock has peaked or hit bottom is difficult even for experienced investors, and for the novice it can be unnerving and financially ruinous.

GET-RICH-QUICK SCHEMES

High income–low net worth investors have a tendency to try to make it big with one financial hit. Make no mistake, these people work hard and are attempting to live the American dream. But because of their interest in maintaining an extravagant lifestyle, they are financially strapped and have little to show for their efforts in terms of net worth. They are not disciplined savers and can't sacrifice present purchases in favor of accumulating a sizeable estate. Many are looking to take an easier road to riches.

In contrast, high-net-worth investors remain secretive about their wealth and investment plans. They also are guarded about financial advice from dubious sources. Recognizing that there is always someone looking to separate them from their money, the high net worth are not receptive to claims of exorbitant returns on invested capital. A conservative lot by nature, they do not mix business with other areas of their life.

The high income–low net worth are more prone to take "insider tips" from friends, acquaintances, and even strangers they meet at social events and clubs.

Joining these same clubs and attending the same social functions are people who prey on the high income–low net worth. These folks look, act, and dress just like their victims. They live in the same upscale neighborhoods, wear expensive clothes and jewelry, have the correct accessories, and drive luxury automobiles. They make a convincing presentation to the unwary.

A member of the high income–low net worth group, Larry A., a director of human resources for an oil services company, remarked to his business associates and other clients he could make them more than 30 percent profit on their money. Responding to a sales pitch from an unregulated financial group, Larry invested his own money, which provided astounding returns for a few months. Having gotten his attention, the investment group asked Larry if he could recruit other people interested in making a lot of money in a relatively short period of time. Needless to say, the profits came to a halt two months later when the illegal pyramid scheme began to unravel. The FBI began to investigate Larry. Since Larry did not directly profit from any of his friends and associates signing up as investors, he was not prosecuted by the government. He was lucky. All he lost was the initial $75,000 investment, another $25,000 he had added a month later, and a few business friends.

In another instance, after being contacted by an outside

private party, Kyle E., a client who worked for an investment publication, sold insider trading information. Kyle made $60,000 and the outside party made several times that much. The Securities and Exchange Commission (SEC) investigated and prosecuted all of the participants in the scheme and Kyle was fired. Kyle was forced to make restitution of the money, pay a heavy fine, and serve a lengthy term of probation.

Whether to invest your money or spend it will clearly be an individual decision based on your lifestyle and priorities. Choosing the former would mean dramatic gains in real estate and the stock market in the years ahead. By paying yourself first, putting that money into investments, and avoiding get-rich-quick schemes, those of you seeking high net worth will be on the path to financial independence.

SIGNPOSTS

FINANCIAL RISK AND SECURITY

Investing guidelines are given for those seeking high net worth.

1. RULE OF 10.

a. Save at least 10 percent of your gross earnings from each paycheck and consistently invest it.

b. Try to increase this rate to 15–20 percent of your gross earnings during your thirties.

c. Finally, attempt to save 20–50 percent of your annual salary at the height of the family's earning power until retirement.

2. POWER OF 72.

a. Divide 72 by the interest rate to obtain the number of years it will take to double your money.

b. Divide 72 by the number of years until maturity to obtain the interest rate needed for doubling your money.

c. Money invested will increase even faster because of compound growth if you reinvest capital gains and dividends as you continue to save more money from your paycheck.

3. THE STOCK MARKET AND MUTUAL FUNDS AS A LONG-TERM INVESTMENT.

a. The stock market has shown a return of 10 percent annually on average since the 1930s.

b. Individual stock purchases and mutual funds are favorites of the high net worth.

c. The high net worth use research to determine what stocks to buy or sell.

4. INDIVIDUAL RETIREMENT ACCOUNTS CAN ALSO MAKE HIGH-NET-WORTH FAMILIES MILLIONAIRES.

a. Investors at certain income levels can deduct the maximum $2,000 IRA contribution from their federal income tax.

b. The maximum $2,000 contribution each year is tax-deferred until the investor turns fifty-nine and a half, or retires. The dividends and interest can also be reinvested without a tax liability until that time.

c. With thirty to forty years' worth of contributions earning 10 percent, it is possible for an investor to have around $400,000–$500,000 and a married couple to accumulate $800,000–$1 million by retirement.

5. REAL ESTATE AS AN INVESTMENT.

a. After purchasing a primary residence, investors can

use their discretionary income to invest in other forms of real estate.

b. Some investors like to buy rental property and raw land. This kind of investment may take more time, research, and know-how than the stock market.

c. Real Estate Investment Trusts (REITs) are also an investment possibility for those who favor real estate as an investment but don't want to own any property themselves.

6. HIGH INCOME–LOW NET WORTH INVESTORS OPERATE DIFFERENTLY THAN THE HIGH NET WORTH.

a. The high income–low net worth place their money in accessible accounts in order to have it available for spending.

b. The high income–low net worth tend to trade stocks often, leading to higher taxes on their gains. Other drawbacks are: very careful bookkeeping is required; they end up paying more for tax preparation services; and they may have to pay estimated taxes if they post large gains.

c. The high income–low net worth have to severely cut back on their expenditures when the economy slows because they have few financial resources at their disposal.

d. High-net-worth families stockpile their money and

watch their investments closely in good times and bad.

7. GET-RICH-QUICK SCHEMES.

a. The high income–low net worth are more susceptible to scams and get-rich-quick schemes.

b. The high net worth are more skeptical of opportunities that sound too good to be true.

5

THE WINNING ATTITUDE

GENERALLY, THE HIGH NET WORTH ARE CARE-ful consumers who have learned how easy it is to fall into debt. They have developed a winning attitude toward money, credit, and budgeting either through trial and error or because they were raised with the proper values. The high-net-worth household saves for the things they need. There is less chance they will buy out of impulse, emotion, or because other people covet a product or device. They rationally calculate the cost-benefit of their purchase and whether the product or service is really useful or needed. They take the time to search out the best quality and price. American companies rightly recognize that if this were the nature of most consumers, their bottom lines would be in big trouble. Fortunately for America's retailers, the high net worth form a minority of consumers.

The high-net-worth household knows that the list price is not necessarily the price they have to pay. They are not opposed to the seller making money on the transaction, but they want to make sure the seller is not exacting an exorbitant profit at their expense. They refuse to pay a premium for a trendy product (such as the new Volkswagen Beetle). They will wait until the supply catches up with demand and then purchase one below sticker price.

The low net worth rationalize the spend-now-save-later trap by telling themselves they are investing in themselves, whether it be a new car, a larger house, designer clothes, or travel. No doubt education and training are invaluable and serve as excellent investments in their own right, but the upshot of increased earnings for the majority of people is more and larger purchases. Rather than save and invest the increased salary and bonuses, they forget everyone needs cash for retirement and economic slowdowns. The money earned today and invested is the source of everything a family will need down the road. A lesson gleaned from the high net worth is that a lifestyle should not mortgage the future. A family must take into account tomorrow's obligations and realities when planning its financial course.

In contrast, low-net-worth households display several distinct characteristics in their purchasing habits. They rarely bargain for the best deal because they are more interested in taking possession of the item as fast as possible. Somehow, they believe bargaining would display an unflattering, unprofessional image. Second, they are afraid others will believe they *need* the price reduced in order to afford the merchandise. They also want to display that they have the means to pay for an expensive new item, since they strive to project upper-class status. Ego-driven needs for attention, recognition, and self-esteem keep the low net worth in a never-ending spiral to acquire more and more, because once a possession is bought the attractiveness quickly wears off.

As an example of the need for status, people who cannot afford expensive new luxury automobiles have turned to purchasing simulated blue headlight bulbs for their low and mid-priced cars. The bulbs create the illusion that their car is equipped with costly lights known as xenon lights. The trend towards xenon lights began in 1995 and they have quickly become synonymous with luxury vehicles. That, in turn, has created an after-market for hordes of status-seekers who cannot afford a costly BMW, Lincoln, or Mercedes but want, nonetheless, to impress the in-crowd.

Projecting upper-class status is not a concern for the high-net-worth consumer. Their primary need is to be financially independent: to have the means to care for their family and to keep their business running. If they work for someone else, it is to look forward to an early retirement so they can place their time in fun endeavors, new interests, and fresh challenges.

CREDIT CARDS

One of the more interesting aspects of the high net worth, in contrast to their low-net-worth counterparts, is that they work the system to make consumers who go into debt pay their way. For example, it is quite easy to obtain a no-fee credit card from a bank or financial institution. If a consumer pays the entire balance, they get to use the bank's money for a month without a charge. Of course this is not what the bank is counting on—the bank wants and expects the consumer to carry a balance each month so they can charge a fee on the unpaid balance. The people who pay the monthly minimum (and there are millions) actually support the high-net-worth person's free use of the card. Should the average consumer change their pattern and begin to pay off their balance each month, banks would begin to charge a monthly fee to all consumers. Department stores operate the same way and have determined that most of their customers keep a monthly balance where interest can be charged. The charge card, therefore, has become a profit center in its own right above and beyond the store's core business.

Unlike high-net-worth households, the high income–low net worth carry large balances on their credit cards and tend to respond to low-rate credit card solicitations that come in the mail. After accepting the teaser rate and taking possession of the new card, they customarily pay little attention to it. Low-rate offers increasingly come with a host of land mines for the unwary that dramatically boost interest and fees. With fifteen days' notice, a credit card company can legally change the rate from an introductory offer of say 1.9–3.9 percent to between 18 and 25 percent, although it can even go as high as 32.6 percent.

In addition to higher interest rates, they can change the terms of the deal. For example, credit card companies can apply punitive charges, such as increased fees for late payments or for exceeding the credit limit. Although they used to give consumers a grace period of thirty days to make a payment before late charges set in, this is often no longer true. Some companies have reduced their closing dates to within two weeks of when the bill is due, and it usually takes the card issuer seven to ten days to process a payment. This means the consumer must pay the bill within a few days of receiving it, or else they risk late charges of thirty dollars or more, as well as the threat of a punitive interest rate increase. Card issuers are also less likely to waive late fees for those consumers who regularly pay their balance in full.

Credit card companies for years have offered their clients checks that encourage them to transfer balances or spend more around the holidays. The temporary low rates are tempting, but buried in the fine print is a new change that allows companies to charge a transaction fee of as much as 3 percent per month for using this check privilege, essentially a "usurious" rate imposed in a legal manner. This in effect doubles the annual interest rate and may compound it indefinitely if the consumer carries a balance from month to month.

If a high income–low net worth household were to decide to terminate the card, closing fees might accrue when the card is canceled. Finally, some companies apply inactivity fees for people who fail to use a card within a set period, such as six months or a year. The charges, punitive and otherwise, are disclosed either in the original credit card agreement or in subsequent statement inserts or notices. By not responding, the recipient accepts the new terms. For the average high income–low net worth household, the accrual of credit card interest on large balances will amount to a significant amount of money. This is not lost on the high net worth, who therefore do not use revolving credit.

The average American family maintains an ongoing debt balance of several thousand dollars accumulating interest at a significant rate of at least 19.8 percent per year. Overall, debt loads remain at or near all-time highs. Personal bankruptcies have increased to record levels; in 1997, 1.33 million filings were posted. The same year, $23.1 billion in total credit card defaults ocurred; nearly half that amount was bankruptcy related. While credit card debt accounts for only about 5 percent of total consumer debt, it is currently the fastest growing area. The percentage of take-home pay spent on nonmortgage debt in the United States has climbed to more than 18 percent, the highest levels since the boom in spending that followed World War II. Credit counselors, as a rule, urge consumers to seek help when their debt load reaches 20 percent of their take-home pay.

The combination of ready credit and personal generosity creates a slippery slope for high income–low net worth households, especially around the holidays and special occasions. In 1998, a survey for Intuit, Inc., makers of Quicken financial software, found that the average female consumer spends $986 during the Christmas season; the average male consumer, $1,023. The average for people in the prime child-rearing ages of thirty-five to forty-four is $1,117. Moreover, the survey discovered that 60 percent of shoppers do not set a holiday budget and another 12 percent set a budget but expect to exceed it.

Credit cards encourage spending. Prior to the 1950s, before the universal appeal of credit cards and direct-mail catalogs, credit was restricted to specific retail stores and retail associations. Credit is far easier to come by in this day and age, and the idea of saving for a rainy day has been discarded like yesterday's newspaper. Unsolicited credit cards, cards available to people with wages barely above the poverty line, and deferred payment plans on major purchases have lulled consumers into a false sense of security.

Industry studies show that the average credit card transaction is larger than cash transactions or debit card sales. The high cost of goods also contributes to consumer spending getting out of control during the Christmas season, traditionally the largest shopping period in the year. Christmas adds between $15 billion and $20 billion to the more than $500 billion Americans already owe on their credit cards.

In the last few years, borrowers have begun taking out home equity loans to pay off their credit card debt. The percentage of home owners with home equity lines of credit has grown from 6 percent in 1988 to 8 percent in 1998. Using home equity to pay off consumer debt can make sense financially, because many home equity loans offer tax breaks and lower rates than the typical credit card. But borrowers put their homes at risk by doing so, increasing the chance that a layoff, a financial setback, or another cycle of credit card splurging could result in a foreclosure.

Financial experts suggest the key to keeping out of high

credit card debt, which is not a problem for the high net worth, is to plan the purchases in advance of shopping.

First, put together a list of people for whom you plan on buying gifts. Then decide how much you are willing to spend on each person. Most people link the name with an item, but this can cause a problem because there is a wide price range for nearly all consumables. People feel obligated to purchase more expensive items when in the heat of shopping, so the amount, not the item, is the operative element.

Second, all of the items on the list should be added to obtain a grand total. If this amount exceeds what you can afford, go back and either adjust the amounts for each person or eliminate someone from the list. Keep paring the list until the total budget is achieved.

Third, drive to the bank or automatic teller machine and draw out the budgeted amount in cash. After that amount is spent, the shopping is completed.

Last, begin thinking about next year's budget in the same manner. People tend to forget their past holiday-season experiences. Typically, it takes the average consumer eight months to pay off the debt accumulated between Thanksgiving and Christmas Eve. Just as they get it paid off, it is holiday season again. This is just as true for Jewish families as it is for Christians. In the past twenty years, Hanukkah has become very commercialized and, with eight days of observance, the gift-giving can easily be as expensive as a Christmas celebration.

After the holiday shopping is over, sit down with the receipts, checkbook, and shopping list to determine what could be done better the next time around. Think about what the grand total will be the next year and divide it by twelve. Each month, put that amount away in a bank or credit union account. Watch pre- and post-holiday sales at department stores and specialty shops for price reductions on clothing and household goods. Christmas decorations and other seasonal items can be purchased for steep discounts during this time as well. If a family has some money left over and can store the items, this can be a good time to stock up for the following year.

The average millionaire has mastered how to use credit appropriately. Most American households own either a MasterCard or Visa and either a department store or gasoline credit card—and the average high-net-worth family is no different. But while most American families also use a multitude of *other* credit cards, the high net worth, on average, have just those two. Instead of maintaining a high balance, the high net worth pay off the balance each month, which means they use credit free of charge at the bank's expense. Financial institutions have long gone after high-net-worth households because they believe they can tap into their discretionary income. If they had done their homework, they would know they will not make money beyond the 3 percentage points merchants pay to use the card's service.

In terms of store-brand credit cards, the authors in *The Millionaire Next Door* found millionaires are more likely to have a Sears or J.C. Penney card than Brooks Brothers. For upscale specialty stores, a small percentage of the wealthy have Neiman Marcus, Saks, Eddie Bauer, or Lord & Taylor cards. For the elitist cards—American Express Platinum, Carte Blanche, and Diner's Club—less than 10 percent of millionaires use them.

A recent marketing trend has been for banks to rebate 1–3 percent of annual purchases back to the consumer's account. This kind of money-back deal is very attractive to high-net-worth households.

CONSUMERISM

Consuming has been the great American pastime since the end of World War II. The television jingles baby boomers grew up with as children encouraged tremendous brand loyalty. What was consumed served as a personal statement for that generation for decades. In the past few years, though, brand loyalty has ebbed and price has become the most important consideration for the average consumer.

Unaffected by the engine of consumption, the high net worth have insulated themselves from Madison Avenue marketing. Make no mistake about it, high-net-worth households are not easily swayed by price alone. Quality of service and the responsiveness of the vendor are also important to them. They will not be persuaded by slick advertising copy. Instead, they talk to friends, neighbors, relatives, and associates to learn who they have used, whether they were satisfied with the level of service, what problems they have encountered, and whether they would recommend the company to others. Networking and referrals work for the high-net-worth household.

In purchasing a product, the high net worth will also investigate what is included in the price, whether it has to be assembled, and what options and accessories are necessary to make it operational. Their decision to buy will depend upon the total cost of purchasing all of the components, reliability, cost of maintenance, and the availability of parts.

Another difference between high-net-worth households and high income–low net worth households concerns technology. The high income–low net worth tend to purchase the newest high-tech gadgets when they first come out. Often the technology is untested and the cost of the product is also high. The high net worth typically wait until the technology has been proven or until the next generation of products have reached the market. This is their pattern in the purchase of computer equipment, stereo systems, VCRs, and TVs. By waiting, they can decide whether a quadraphonic or dual speaker system will be in vogue, whether Beta or the half-inch VCR will be the standard accepted by the public, or whether compact discs (CDs) will dominate the market over long-playing vinyl records.

Another issue is product quality. Many high-net-worth households ask around and network regarding the quality of products in which they are interested. But their research does not stop there. They will check out *Consumer Reports* and other consumer-oriented publications for ratings and rankings, as well as ask questions at retail stores in gathering information for a major purchase. High-net-worth purchasers spend the time necessary to make a well-informed choice.

The first generation of any new product usually has defects and deficiencies. With intense competition, short market lead-times, and rapid advances in technology, companies are often releasing new products before all of the flaws are removed.

High-net-worth households plan purchases well in advance. If they buy a big-ticket item, they put cash down, as earnest money, and pay the remainder upon delivery. They look for discounts, coupons, special sales, markdowns, rebates and buy in quantity or bulk. They are willing to buy off-brand or generic labels if the quality is there. They are also willing to negotiate cost. The high net worth are not afraid to ask a clerk or sales professional whether the store will match the price of a competitor should they find the same product on sale elsewhere for less. Should the store lower its price in a given time frame, say thirty days, they will ask the store to refund the difference in the form of cash, store credit, or a rebate to their credit card. In a word, they are *cautious* about how they spend their income.

High-net-worth families are continually looking for the best value for the dollars they are willing to spend. They are not afraid to exchange failed products for store credit or a refund. High-net-worth families want to deal with companies that willingly accept returns and exchanges of defective or questionable merchandise. Moreover, they are more apt to buy imperfect goods, such as car tires and clothing sold as "blems."

High income–low net worth households spend on what is fashionable and in style, rather than depend on quality, service, or a return policy. They are usually less price sensitive and less willing to go out of their way to look for bargains. Even if something is defective, they are more interested in an exchange than servicing or their money back. If the item is already out of date, they would just as soon buy a new model.

SIGNPOSTS

THE WINNING ATTITUDE
The high net worth are careful in their use of credit cards and in purchasing consumer goods and services. They do not throw away their money.

1. THE HIGH INCOME–LOW NET WORTH ARE WILLING TO GO INTO DEBT TO PURCHASE SOUGHT-AFTER ITEMS, AND THEY DO NOT LIKE TO BARGAIN.

a. They see bargaining as unprofessional. Plus, they don't want to wait for something they desire right now.

b. Bargaining gives the false impression that they need the price to be reduced in order to afford the merchandise.

c. They enjoy showing they have the means to afford an expensive new item because it projects the upper-class status they seek.

2. CREDIT CARDS

a. The high net worth carry no more than two credit cards, one of which is usually a card that offers a rebate. As a general rule, they do not own specialty-store cards.

b. The high net worth pay off the cards on time each month and, in effect, make the consumers who don't do so pay their way.

c. The high income–low net worth and low net worth have high revolving credit on multiple cards, and consequently, a high debt load.

d. The average consumer generally takes eight months to pay off their Christmas shopping bills. Some take out equity lines of credit on their home that can put their house in jeopardy.

e. Budgeting can keep the high income–low net worth and the low net worth out of trouble, especially around the Christmas season.

3. THE HIGH NET WORTH SAVE FOR THINGS THEY NEED AND PAY CASH.

a. They do not purchase out of impulse or emotion.

b. The high net worth rationally calculate the cost-benefit of each purchase.

c. They look for discounts, coupons, special sales, markdowns, rebates, and buy generic brands.

d. In many cases, price alone is not the most important consideration.

e. They are willing to pay a fair market price, but they are not willing to pay a premium for scarce commodities.

f. Service, quality of workmanship, and the company's responsiveness to consumers are important.

g. The high net worth network with relatives, friends, associates, and neighbors. They check out consumer-oriented periodicals for information and reviews.

h. They do not purchase recently released high-tech gadgets. They wait until the bugs have been worked out and the cost of the product has dropped.

i. Warranties and guaranties are important.

6

THE ROAD LESS TRAVELED

HIGH-NET-WORTH FAMILIES VALUE MODERA-
tion and, generally, take a middle path in life. The high
net worth are not influenced by what others do or think,
and can best be described as being their own persons.
They are more willing to travel the road of moderation
that accumulates affluence than the road that most other
people journey.

The low net worth, and to a greater degree the high
income–low net worth, do not display a similar financial
focus. They are easily tugged and pulled in different directions. Their early experience with consumption orients
them towards comfort and indulging in physical delights
and desires. This characteristic fits the great majority of the
American buying public. The high net worth make a con-
certed effort to protect themselves from complacency and
from becoming too comfortable in their outward success.

HEALTH

The high net worth take care of themselves. They are more interested in prevention than in dealing with disease and illness after the fact. They are moderate in what they eat and drink, consume what is reasonably good for them, and meet regularly with a doctor and dentist. They tend to smoke less than other economic groups and drink alcohol with restraint. In part, this is because they value moderation for its own sake. To them, a habit does not seem a reasonable condition to support. They also feel that spending money on a habit or addiction demonstrates a serious lack of control. Feeling in control and taking responsibility for their actions are two of the most conspicuous characteristics of the high net worth.

Low-net-worth and high income–low net worth families watch what other people are doing. They indulge their tastes by dining out often. The high income–low net worth are also more apt to engage in gourmet cooking. Interestingly, they also buy the most recent diet books. If you were to visit their homes, you would probably find diet books and cookbooks standing next to one another on the kitchen counter. They also sign up for expensive gym plans, buy home exercise equipment, engage personal trainers, and purchase the latest sportswear. Rather than being interested in the benefits of exercise per se, they want to look good and be involved in whatever others consider to be in vogue. Outside the home, the high income–low net worth want to look the best they can. Inside the home, the tendency is to read, watch television, or view a big-screen video of a workout while exercising—anything to escape the tedium of a stationary bicycle, skiing machine, or rower.

In contrast, the high net worth find physical activities they participate in several times a week. This may or may not require a workout at home. Many dedicated exercisers say they work out not just for their body but also for their mind. In our high-stress society, slamming tennis balls, shooting hoops, or stepping out for a walk or jog are all socially acceptable ways to relieve tension and adjust attitude—just as grandma knew when she advised taking out your anger on the woodpile. Exercise helps regulate biorhythms, which improves sleep and enhances energy level and vigor. It is also very important in maintaining physical health and controlling weight, which impacts one's self-esteem. And exercise improves mental health, helping to elevate mood, reduce anxiety, and enhance one's self-image.

By midlife, the high income–low net worth demonstrate the desire to return to their youth, and legions of corrective surgery specialists and plastic surgeons have earned a comfortable living by solving their cosmetic issues. Not being as vain or self-absorbed, the high net worth generally shun corrective eye surgery, hair restoration, liposuction, and the like.

The high income–low net worth are also more likely to engage in natural remedies and wellness techniques. They tend to purchase copious amounts of vitamins, minerals, and herbal compounds to counteract specific health conditions. Being more traditional in their health care needs, the high net worth predictably show concern about untested procedures and products.

SHOPPING

The high net worth, as a group, show different character-istics as consumers than the high income–low net worth. High-net-worth families are not impulse buyers for one. They are not sensitive to specials or discounts unless they are in the market for the item. A second difference is qual-ity. Frequently, high-net-worth households decide to pur-chase a more expensive item because they have found it will last. They understand that the proverb "you get what you pay for" is true.

Third, the high net worth are not receptive to trends, fads, or gimmicks in their purchases. Until a "new" or "improved" product has weathered the test of time, high-net-worth households use a product with which they are already familiar. A fourth major differ-ence is keeping to a budget. After knowing why they want to purchase something, high-net-worth families will know what they want, how much they are willing to spend, where they want to purchase it, and when they will buy it. High income–low net worth families are more likely to buy whenever they pull together a few discretionary dollars.

Fifth, high-net-worth families buy replacements for devices that break and can no longer be repaired or would be too expensive to fix. The high income–low net worth, above all, look to spend on the trendy and new to further enhance their prestige in the neighborhood. They also tend to change appliances when they replace their decor. Sixth, the high net worth visit stores for the purpose of inspecting and buying merchandise only when they have to.

High income–low net worth consumers use shopping

in much the same way an alcoholic uses alcohol or an addict uses drugs. They seek escape from inner emptiness, ennui, alienation, and turmoil. Of course, compulsive spending will never solve their problems, but it can certainly create more of them.

RECREATION

The high net worth, by and large, are rather conservative in their recreational and leisure activities. Exceptions to any rule can be found, and no doubt there are people from all walks of life engaging in extreme sports and life-defying exertions, but the high net worth are more likely to enjoy themselves at a ski lodge with a hot drink than risk being on top of a mountain when it is four degrees below zero.

They do not risk life and limb in order to get the feeling they are living life to the fullest. The high net worth rarely spend money to have the wits scared out of them or take a risk that may result in a less-than-pleasurable outcome.

Frank G., the president of a manufacturing company and a man with more than $10 million in net worth, bought identical new black Turbo Carrera Porsches for himself and his wife. Unlike the average high-net-worth investor, Frank was an adrenaline-seeking sports enthusiast. His automobile, a thoroughbred sports racer detuned for the street, had more capability than Frank's driving skills could harness. He and his wife enrolled in a four-day course at Sears Point Raceway in northern California to learn how to handle the car at high speed. Frank quickly realized how dangerous a car of such remarkable power and handling could be at peak-performance driving in an uncontrolled environment. So he decided that when he felt the urge to drive hard, he would take it out only on solo runs at a nearby racetrack.

The high net worth attempt to separate work from play, unlike the high income–low net worth who try to blend the two during cocktail parties and golf dates—or who else are such workaholics that they have no time for leisure activities. The high income–low net worth who use social get-togethers to engage in business do not get a sense of having recreational time; they are merely conducting business in a different environment. Since they are always performing, they suffer continuous stress. The activity can be expensed as a cost of doing business, but the separation of work and play has been lost.

The high net worth who work for companies and corporations grasp the need to develop interests outside of work and the necessity to prevent physical and emotional exhaustion. High-net-worth entrepreneurs place extraordinary pressure on themselves to do well in business, and they tend to treat their enterprise as a hobby. They work hard to make their business successful, love what they do, and spend an inordinate amount of time at work. Contrary to how most people tend to view small business owners, they do not ordinarily have the luxury to leave work when they want, take long vacations several times a year, or entrust the business to non-family members. They realize there will be a high price to pay in their physical and mental well-being if they do not take time out to get away from business and unwind.

As in many other areas of life, the high net worth do not spend excessively on recreation. They are not likely to purchase equipment such as jet skis, snowmobiles, ski equipment, and motorcycles. They are more likely to rent what they need when they vacation. The high income–low net worth usually are the people who buy boats and watercraft. The high net worth typically do not buy vacation homes or time-share condos either. They prefer to rent or lease resort condos, or wangle invitations from their high income–low net worth friends who own places at desirable vacation spots. If they are in the market for a resort home or recreational vehicle, the high net worth are usually ready to retire and hit the road.

TRAVEL

Here, too, the high net worth are moderate in their approach. Unless they are using frequent-flier miles, they do not usually book first-class seats. They may travel off-season and are not opposed to having less than the finest accommodations. As they are paying for their own trip, they are interested only in finding suitable shelter at the most reasonable cost.

The high net worth are likely to purchase a package tour unless the destination is a familiar one. If they are senior citizens, they will take advantage of discounts and will even fly standby. As in so many other areas, their main concern is a fair value for the money spent. The high income–low net worth, on the other hand, spend their time at the very best lodgings and travel first class to fulfill their need for social status.

High-net-worth tourists purchase what is useful and functional for a trip: clothes, film for a camera or camcorder, camping equipment (if they are going to rough it), and toiletries. The high income–low net worth have a propensity to bring along what is trendy and attractive to thieves, such as jewelry and large amounts of cash. The high net worth leave jewelry at home and bring only credit cards, a driver's license, and travelers checks. What valuables they do bring they carry on board the flight.

High income–low net worth families arrange vacations during the summer, when their children are out of school. They pay a premium for traveling during this peak time of year—no bargains here. In order to save, the high-net-worth family will go either before or after the peak summer tourist season. To conserve cash, they will also look for more offbeat destinations than what their high income–low net worth counterparts would normally consider.

As an illustration, Bill and Sue, a high-net-worth corporate couple, arranged for Sue's mother to watch their little boy so they could go on an extended vacation, booking a flight in the off-season (early October) to London with a return from Frankfurt, Germany, a month later. Since they were traveling when school was in session and American tourists had already taken their summer vacation, they found air travel at a reasonable cost.

After arriving in London and touring for a few days, Bill and Sue arranged for a rental car once they traveled on to France. Because they visited during the off-season, they did not have to worry about booking bed-and-breakfast accommodations in advance. This way they could travel in a spontaneous fashion rather than be tied to a schedule arranged months in advance. Overall, they found that the rates were 20–30 percent less expensive than during peak summer times, and they spent the remainder of the month wandering in a carefree manner throughout Western Europe.

High-net-worth corporate personnel schedule vacations and travel to coincide with business trips. This may entail use of the corporate jet, company car (mileage, gas and oil, and insurance are paid for by the firm), hotel stay for the family at a corporate discount, a visit at a resort in the company's name, and so forth. In addition, sales personnel are often in a position to benefit from company perks. Many organizations pay entirely for trips won by employees in sales contests. Companies often encourage sales staff to bring their families along to regional and national meetings, where the company arranges dinners, dances, an awards banquet, and special events for spouses only.

The only area where moderation is not a virtue to the high-net-worth family is in their financial investing. High-net-worth families withhold 20–50 percent or more of their discretionary income for investment in stocks, mutual funds, and real estate. They know exactly where their financial priorities lie and, as we'll see in the next chapter, they are not afraid to spend good money in the present if it will reap big rewards in later life.

SIGNPOSTS

THE ROAD LESS TRAVELED
The high-net-worth family values moderation.

1. HOW THE HIGH NET WORTH TREAT THEIR HEALTH.

a. The high net worth take care of themselves physically.

b. They are moderate in food and drink.

c. They do not subscribe to health fads, elective surgery for cosmetic reasons, or natural remedies or wellness techniques.

d. They consider exercising and conditioning important.

e. They seek out more than one medical opinion for diagnosis and treatment.

2. HOW THE HIGH NET WORTH DEAL WITH SHOPPING AND PURCHASES.

a. The high net worth are not impulsive buyers.

b. They look for quality and are willing to pay for merchandise that will last.

c. They are not receptive to trends or gimmicks.

d. The high net worth keep to a budget.

e. They tend to buy replacements for items that break and cannot be repaired or are too expensive to fix.

f. They shop only when they need to.

g. They buy in quantity.

3. HOW THE HIGH NET WORTH DEAL WITH RECREATIONAL PURSUITS.

a. The high net worth are conservative in their recreational and leisure activities.

b. They are more apt to rent equipment than to buy it outright. They are more likely to rent or lease vacation accommodations than to buy time-share condos or vacation homes.

c. They try to separate work from play in order to use leisure activities to unwind and rest.

d. They are normally not adrenaline-seeking risk takers.

4. HOW THE HIGH NET WORTH DEAL WITH TRAVEL.

a. The high net worth look for discounts on airline flights or fly standby.

b. They travel off-season and receive greater savings this way.

c. They will negotiate package tours in order to obtain exactly what they want.

d. The corporate high net worth might schedule vacations to coincide with business trips.

e. They look for reasonable, not upper-class, accommodations.

f. They bring only what is useful and functional for a trip.

g. They do not bring expensive jewelry or take large sums of cash with them.

h. The high net worth do not purchase expensive designer luggage that helps thieves and burglars target them.

7

THE TRAVELING TEAM

BY AND LARGE, MOST PEOPLE DO NOT REVIEW where they are or where they are going financially on a regular basis. Not getting expert advice on your money is a *huge* mistake.

The low net worth who have not consistently and diligently pursued personal investing tend to fall into three categories. First, those who wait until their fifties or sixties to begin saving and investing. By then they have to invest large amounts each year to hit their target. Second, those who decide to live to the hilt and enjoy the fruits of their labor now. If they do not have a pension from their employer, these folks will be forced to work until the end. Third, those who invest up to a point, but not enough to prevent part-time work in their later retirement years.

People in these three groups would not hesitate to see

a physician for a physical complaint, a dentist for a toothache, or a lawyer to protect their legal interests. But for some reason, they do not feel a pressing need to regularly seek out professional help to enhance and protect their financial position. So there are millions of people trying to handle their own investments without a clue.

Compounding the problem are a spate of self-help books on personal finance. Investors without a firm foundation in this arena cannot differentiate between various strategies in order to find the correct one for their circumstances.

An investor just getting started has a very steep learning curve ahead. There are two ways to learn: from one's own mistakes or from the mistakes of others. Certainly, there is less wear and tear, and less financial exposure, in learning from others. But picking up an understanding of investing cannot be accomplished in a weekend by reading a book or two.

Because of the complexity of today's financial markets, it is very important to have trusted advisors who make their living in investing. A financial advisor is vital because he or she can suggest, advise, instruct, and be a sounding board once an investor is up to speed.

Personal financial advice as a corporate perk is relatively new. Only in the past twenty years have companies provided financial planning for their key senior executives. Some firms have set up financial planning sessions with an advisor of the company's choosing. More commonly, however, the executive will search out their own assistance, with the company paying the bill. Recently, consultants calling themselves counselors, mentors, or coaches have sprung up to fill this need for senior executives.

Today, executives at all stages of net worth have started to imitate how the high net worth build a team of advisors. The high net worth like to bring together professionals from a number of disciplines to assist in their areas of specific expertise. Members of this "traveling team" might include a stockbroker, a certified financial planner, a chartered financial analyst, or a registered investment advisor; a certified public accountant; possibly a tax attorney, a number of insurance agents, and a banker. The investor needs to know what can be expected from each and must become well informed enough to ask the right questions. These advisors' combined experience and advice will be invaluable for the investor planning to build a net worth of $1 million.

The best place to begin searching for members of a traveling team of advisors is with family, business associates, and trusted friends. Ask those whose investment knowledge you respect the most who they recommend. You can also talk to your certified public accountant, tax preparer, or lawyer, if you should have one. They usually know firsthand which advisors make money for clients. Another suggestion is to get in touch with professional associations and obtain their recommendations. Watch for announcements of free investment workshops and seminars in the local newspapers. Check these out, but be careful. Never entrust your money to people you have not thoroughly investigated, and make sure they are local.

Cary R., a vice president of sales for an East Coast

software company, was contacted by a financial planner out of Chicago. Cary inquired how the planner learned about him. The advisor stated that he had gotten Cary's name off a list from a professional association to which Cary belonged. The planner stated that he only worked with professionals in the computer industry and had a marvelous track record of making them money. Cary was neither impressed nor interested. He mentioned that working with a financial professional so far away made as much sense as traveling to Chicago for a dental checkup. Cary wanted to be as close to his financial advisor and his money as he could. This is extremely valuable advice.

STOCKBROKERS

Licensed by the Securities and Exchange Commission (SEC), stockbrokers are uniquely qualified to assist new investors in generating wealth. They spend their time trying to uncomplicate the massive choice of investment products in the marketplace for the average investor.

The stockbroker performs four important tasks. First, stockbrokers will assist clients in determining their long-term financial goals and a time frame for achieving them. Without an idea of what the clients are aiming for and how many years until they retire, there is no way to formulate an investment strategy. Second, they help determine the level of risk—speculative, high growth, moderate growth, conservative growth, or income—clients can handle. Individual circumstances, age, income, and the investor's personality usually determine the amount of appropriate risk. Based on historical data, the rate of return over time in any category will indicate how quickly it might take to reach the target. Third, stockbrokers can help determine and recommend stocks and mutual funds that are compatible with the risk factor investors are willing to assume. Fourth and last, they can set up investment accounts, IRAs, and the purchase of individual stocks and mutual funds.

Stockbrokers are paid by commission for buying and selling stocks. Commissions usually range from 1.5 percent on stock trades to 8.5 percent on mutual funds and other packaged products. Since most brokers work for large stockbrokerages, many times they tout certain issues because the commissions are higher. For this reason, many investment experts feel that commission-based investment advice generates too many conflicts of interest. The individual investor must make sure that the stock being touted fits in with the investment strategy already laid out.

Usually, the high net worth who work best with stockbrokers are knowledgeable about the market. They have been savvy investors for many years and make choices based on long-range strategy. They tend to use a stockbroker as a source of new ideas and a sounding board on the latest trends. A stockbroker is in a good position to see the market on an everyday basis, to be able to point out inconsistencies in strategy, and to caution the investor about potential problems. For example, Harry R., an executive in the automotive industry, received a caution from his broker that, because his net worth had surpassed $1.2 million, he should change his retirement and resource management accounts from a joint tenancy with his wife to a trust, in order to avoid unnecessary taxation on the estate.

Unless they work in the financial planning industry, most investors do not have the ability to devote a lot of time to evaluating market trends, researching new investments, and tracking their portfolio. So a majority of high-net-worth investors count on a trusted advisor who can keep them apprised of trends in the marketplace. High-net-worth investors find it advisable to discuss their various investment accounts at least once or twice a year to determine what should be bought or sold then, what should be purchased in the following year, and what new financial instruments might be worth investigating for future investment purposes.

Investors who have not had much experience in financial markets may need more assistance in devising a financial strategy. Investment advisors are typically independent and have a fiduciary responsibility for the clients' portfolios. This means they make investment decisions on behalf of the client based upon the individual client's objectives. Certified financial planners, chartered financial analysts, and registered investment advisors all can devise in-depth long-range financial strategies and keep up-to-date in how the investments are tracking.

CERTIFIED FINANCIAL PLANNERS
The Certified Financial Planner (CFP) designation is offered by the College of Financial Planning. Aspiring

planners attend a three-year program that often can be completed in one year. They also must keep abreast in the field by taking continuing education credits. CFPs can be stockbrokers, mutual fund salespeople, or insurance agents. Certified financial planners are registered with the SEC, so they can recommend as well as purchase stocks or mutual funds through stockbrokerages. Their advisement and recommendation process works the same as an investor dealing with a stockbroker. They need to know an investor's financial goal and time frame, and what risk an investor is willing to assume. Then the CFP can set up accounts and make investments agreed upon with the client. Oftentimes, they recommend specific products they have bought for their own portfolio or the portfolio of other clients. Dealing from extensive experience, they are in a position to discuss the pros and cons of specific courses of action. CFPs are also in a position to develop and implement a comprehensive financial strategy. The plan can include how much to save, how much to budget, how much insurance to buy, how to save on income taxes, and how to save for college.

CFPs can either be fee-only or non-fee-only advisors. Unlike stockbrokers, who accept a commission on purchasing or selling individual stocks or mutual funds, CFPs who are fee-only receive payment based on an hourly rate, usually ranging between $100–$200 per hour. A comprehensive plan could easily cost upwards of $5,000–$10,000, but the cost is well worth it.

CHARTERED FINANCIAL ANALYSTS

The Chartered Financial Analyst (CFA) has concluded a three-year course developed and implemented by the Institute of Chartered Financial Analysts. It is a more comprehensive designation than that of a certified financial planner, although the CFA performs the same functions. In the long run, the more academic designation may or may not indicate the better money manager for your specific needs. CFAs tend to favor conventional portfolio strategies over new ones, and therefore work best with conservative investors.

REGISTERED INVESTMENT ADVISORS

A third category of investment professional is the Registered Investment Advisor (RIA). This advisor is governed by the SEC and the state securities department. Like the CFP and CFA, the registered investment advisor is paid in one of three ways: by fee-only (flat rate based on assets managed or time), by commission (based on the amount of the purchase), or by a combination of fees and commissions.

Although there are advisors who receive commissions and fees, it is generally felt that, as I mentioned earlier, commission-based investment advice from such sources can present a conflict of interest. It is prudent for an investor to find an RIA who fits one of two types of fee-only advisors: money managers or financial planners.

Fee-only financial planners make investment decisions for their clients based on risk tolerance and the client's goals. They are normally compensated by a fee that is based on the total amount of money they handle.

Fee-only money managers provide more services than money managers but are paid the same, based on the total value of the account. In addition to investments, they can help investors with budgeting, taxes, life insurance, real estate, retirement planning, and estate planning. For that work, the investor can negotiate a yearly retainer. On smaller estates, they are paid a fee based on the amount of time it takes to put a plan together. The fees range from $150 to $200 an hour, which is comparable to a CFP.

A good strategy for an investor would be to contract with either a CFP, CFA, or RIA, plus have a stockbroker to give opinions on new instruments. Also, the stockbroker can be invaluable in maintaining a watchful eye on the market and the investor's portfolio on an everyday basis.

SELECTING A CFP, CFA, OR AN RIA

A knowledgeable investor should be concerned with finding an investment advisor who has technical expertise, a shared investment philosophy, the proper education, credentialing, and training—and someone with whom they feel comfortable. Interview at least three to five people before making a decision. Investors may differ as to the importance of any particular factor but the following list will help in comparing different candidates:

1. Ask the advisor to give a brief overview of their early years, work history, and current endeavors.

2. Find out where and when they went to college. Inquire about any advanced degrees or special certifications. A college education will show perseverance and tenacity. If you are in doubt, ask them to prove they have a degree (an official college transcript will do). But you should not base your decision solely on whether or not the advisor has a degree. If the candidate did not finish college, make sure they can demonstrate at least five years of investment experience. If you are willing to work with a relative newcomer, invest only a small amount of money at first.

3. Inquire whether the candidate keeps up in the field with continuing education credits. Find out where and when they have attended any courses, workshops, and seminars.

4. Learn about their employment history in depth. Watch out for frequent job hoppers or people who have a hard time explaining many changes in a short period. This may demonstrate a lack of maturity, perseverance, or questionable business practices. If they are working for themselves, ask when and why they left their former employer. The best advisor is someone who has experienced at least one big market correction, such as the one in October 1987.

5. Find out how many clients they serve. On the one hand, if the money manager or financial advisor has too many clients, they may be too busy and not be available for phone consultations or in-person meetings. On the

other hand, if they have too few clients, they may not have much experience. Up to a limit, the more clients, the more experience. If you are looking for an advisor who has the widest possible experience, you should find out the total worth of the portfolios they control. An advisor with more than $25 million under their management is handling a fairly significant amount.

6. It is a good idea to ask each candidate for three current clients who could serve as references. Be aware that the advisors will only use clients who will give favorable testimonials, so it will be up to the investor to ask questions to get as much information as possible from them. Possible questions to ask include:

a. How long have you known the advisor? How did you meet or who referred you? How long have you worked with your advisor?

b. Have you been satisfied with the service or help so far? Why or why not?

c. How much money have you made listening to their advice? How was your portfolio performance each quarter for the last few years?

d. What do you look for in working with an advisor? How have they met your criteria?

e. How many times do you meet and what do you discuss?

f. Are they available on short notice? At the end of the year do you go over the year-end results and the strategy for the following year?

g. If you could change anything, what would you modify in your investment advice, strategy, or relationship with the advisor? What do you like best and least about your advisor?

h. Did the advisor follow through on the services, advice, and expertise promised?

i. Knowing what you know now, would you hire the advisor again? Why or why not?

7. Find out how the advisor is compensated.

a. Fee-only compensation is based on a percentage rate. It is common to pay 1.6 percent annually for an account less than $250,000 in total net worth and 1 percent for an account more than $1 million. The fees are negotiable, so it is possible to ask for a discount.

b. Comparing an advisor who is paid a commission is difficult because of the multitude of investment products. Try to compare the commission on a hundred shares of a specific blue-chip stock at the current market rate. You should also inquire about a minimum commission amount, since brokerages differ in this regard.

c. Watch out for hidden costs. For example, an under-writing fee is typically added to a new stock issue or investment product. If there is no commission charge on these, the total underwriting fee could exceed 6 percent. Since stocks or mutual funds are being transferred and exchanged, someone has to pay for the service.

As a further example, if a commission-based broker recommends a mutual fund, ask how the commission is paid. If the broker replies that the fund pays the commission, recognize that many of these funds pay the broker "trailers" that are extra commission payments intended as an incentive to keep clients in the funds. It is in the investor's best interest to pay the commission and not be held captive. As a final example, listen to how a commission-based broker explains his position and ask them to explain 12(b)(1) fees. The "12(b)(1)" is a securities regulation that allows mutual funds to charge a fee in addition to the management fee for such things as marketing, distribution, or sales expenses. These expenses, in essence, disguise a commission. Be sure to avoid 12(b)(1) fees in excess of .25 percent.

8. Have the advisor disclose all the costs involved in each investment. There are additional fees you need to be aware of that do not go to the broker or advisor.

a. Management fees charged by the mutual fund man-agers are one example. Domestic stock mutual funds charge a 1 percent fee, foreign funds are slightly higher, and bond funds charge lower fees.

b. Custodian fees are also common. These are charged by the brokerage firm for holding your account. If the advisor is paid a fee and uses a brokerage firm for trades, you need to be aware of the commission and transaction fees charged by the brokerage.

c. Find out how much it will cost to move an account to another firm. For example, for transferring an IRA, a full service brokerage firm charges a 2 percent penalty or $100, whichever is less.

9. Find out about the advisor's investment philosophy and level of risk tolerance. Also ask what types of clients they work best with. If their orientation is more conservative or more speculative than your own, ask how they plan to reconcile this.

10. Ask about the advisor's specialty and what they think they do best.

11. Find out why they chose the investment business. The answer should include more than the standard cliches, as in "I like people." People usually like to do what interests them and what they are good at. The corollary is also true: people are good at and get the best results in what interests them most.

12. Inquire about the services they or their firm offer. The level of client services often differs among firms and advisors.

13. Call your state's securities department to find out if there have been any complaints filed against the advisor or firm. Traditionally, most consumer complaints involve financial planners, brokers, and advisors who earn their income solely by commissions, particularly those who represent only one company.

CERTIFIED PUBLIC ACCOUNTANT/PUBLIC ACCOUNTANT

These experts are critical in helping lower exposure to business as well as individual taxes. A Certified Public Accountant (CPA) is trained specifically to work with large companies. One of the requirements for certification is to be employed in an accounting capacity for a certain number of hours in a public company. A CPA also has to pass a difficult state board examination. A Public Accountant (PA), although not having rigorous training in large companies as a requirement for certification, fits in well as an advisor for the high-net-worth family and is a little less expensive in terms of hourly fees.

Federal, state, and municipal taxes taken together represent the lion's share from a wage earner's gross income. For most families, the home mortgage represents the single largest expenditure a household makes each month and the interest on the mortgage is one of the largest tax deductions, along with the state property tax, on the federal tax form. A professional accountant can help a family legally minimize their taxes by looking for deductions, credits, allowable gifts and contributions, and long-term capital gains and losses. Their business is to keep abreast of changes in the federal and state tax codes and to pass this information along to the investor. Money saved on taxes can be invested for a greater return.

Almost without exception, high-net-worth households employ a CPA or PA. They help foresee and solve existing problems, assist in planning for their client's future, maintain financial statements, assist in setting up a financial strategy and goals, offer second opinions, and can refer other professionals on an as-needed basis.

As with a financial advisor, it is a good idea to interview from three to five candidates. Questions that can be used in selecting the right CPA or PA include:

1. Inquire whether the CPA or PA is currently licensed in your state. Their diploma may be hanging on a wall in their office.

2. Ask whether they specialize in a particular type of tax work. If you own a small or medium-sized business, it would be worthwhile to find someone who understands the needs and problems of small business owners. If you own a corporation or are engaged in a partnership, look for people with that kind of experience as well as investment knowledge.

3. Find out how long they have been in business and their current client load. As a general rule, it is helpful if they have had a minimum of five years experience. If you own a business or have a partnership, they should have experience with start-ups, fast-growing businesses, and turnarounds. For corporations, having

some understanding or training in organizational change would be helpful.

4. Find out whether the professional or staff will be doing the actual work. If they have a staff, find out how many and the areas of expertise for each. Interview the person or persons who will be working on your tax return, financial statement, or financial plan.

5. Find out whether there is an hourly rate or a flat fee. Most CPAs and PAs charge by the hour, but there are variances. For example, it is appropriate to expect an hourly fee for monthly financial statements and business advice, and a flat fee for preparing tax returns.

6. Ask how accessible they will be. Usually it is necessary to meet during the tax season and once or twice during the year to go over investments.

7. Ask the CPA or PA how they can help reduce the tax burden. You will learn their philosophy and if they have specific strategies based on your current financial situation.

8. Discuss setting up a letter of agreement with the CPA or PA. In this device, the professional will be spelling out in detail the range of services offered, the attendant fees, and how they are derived (flat fee, hourly fee, or a percent of return).

9. Ask for a list of three to five client references. Call

them and set up a telephone or a face-to-face conversation at a mutually convenient time. Ask the references what they like and dislike about their CPA or PA's work. Find out how accessible they have been, whether they seem too busy or stretched, and whether they have followed through on their promises. Ask whether they are a good listener and if they are willing to help out in a lot of different financial areas.

TAX ATTORNEYS

In a more aggressive way than a CPA or PA, a tax attorney can be a big help in legally minimizing taxes. They are particularly appropriate for assisting medium- to large-sized businesses that have a more complex financial structure, substantial international trade, or multiple locations in a number of states.

The high net worth also can benefit from such advisement. As a greater amount of wealth accrues, the high-net-worth family encounters a more involved investment and tax picture. Those involved in the sale of a large cash-generating asset like a small business or commercial real estate can use their advice. Even a small percentage change in tax saved can be translated into a significant dollar figure when large sums are involved. A tax attorney is aware of subtleties in the tax codes and the latest court cases and Internal Revenue Service (IRS) rulings. They are a strong hedge in preventing a high-net-worth household from paying more than their fair share in taxes.

Some attorneys who specialize in taxes also have

developed a practice assisting clients with their investments. They may be registered with the SEC, perhaps have a CFP, CFA, or RIA designation, or a real estate license. The benefit here is that an advisor who has an understanding of and expertise in financial planning and investments, and has the ability to interpret IRS codes and regulations, becomes a one-stop shop. Such an advisor can place financial considerations and their legal implications under one umbrella. The hourly fee for such advisement may be higher, though. As with other advisors, a good way to find one is through professional referral.

Another area for a tax attorney is trusts. There are many different types of trusts, and although it is convenient to consult a lawyer, other people may be competent to give advice as well. The typical trust sets up an account where assets are placed for the benefit of the owner or the heirs. The appointed trustee and beneficiaries have the benefit of property ownership without the responsibility of managing the property.

One area of trusts where mistaken information is commonly found is the living trust. Many people erroneously believe that living trusts can help avoid income or estate taxes. By definition, a living trust is a legal device designed to avoid the costs of probate, a court process that occurs after death and establishes the validity of a will. Living trusts, by themselves, do not avoid taxes, and probate costs can be avoided or minimized with other estate-planning techniques. Be advised that anyone who prepares estate-planning documents should have several years' experience in the field and specialized training.

The "unified credit against gift and estate taxes" is an IRS rule that states that, as of 1999, a single parent can leave behind after death up to $650,000, and two parents combined can leave $1.3 million, without the recipients having to pay estate or gift taxes. In the year 2000, the figures go up to $675,000 for an individual and $1.35 million for a husband and wife. Some documents, such as a will or a simple living trust, can be drawn up using self-help books or software. But it is a good idea for a person with assets worth more than $650,000 ($1.3 million for a couple) or those with complicated estates to seek competent legal advice rather than trying a do-it-yourself approach.

INSURANCE AGENTS

Besides reducing the exposure to unnecessary taxation, another safeguard to the dissipation of wealth is the protection from unforeseen events such as fire, accident, and burglary. To this end, insurance agents are important members of any traveling team. They can help a high-net-worth household reduce their financial risk by identifying plans with appropriate coverage at the lowest cost.

Needless to say, the lowest-cost product or instrument is not always the best. It may be more relevant to consider the number and amount of claims that a company pays out in a given year, the coverage offered, how responsive the firm is in resolving claims, and whether the insurance provisions have changed or been curtailed in the recent past. A call to the state's department of insurance can detail any complaints or actions taken against a particular company or agent. Check with friends, relatives, and professionals about what insurance companies and agents they use.

Home owner's insurance is the first line of protection for a home. Mortgage companies expect home owners to carry enough insurance to pay off the mortgage in the event of a catastrophe. If the policy lapses, they will issue one that costs up to ten times what a home owner could purchase on the open market. Make sure that you keep your home owner's insurance coverage at all times, and if you should change insurance carriers, make sure they provide the mortgage company a copy of your policy, otherwise you might find yourself billed for a very expensive new policy.

A home owner owns both the constructed home and land. Since land cannot easily be destroyed, it is advisable to get an insurance policy that covers only the construction costs of the home and its contents. Make sure the policy has an escalator clause that will take inflation into account. In areas with high housing costs, the land is usually about 40 percent of the home's total value. Check with the insurance company regarding how much it will cost per square foot to rebuild a home in case of a total loss. It may be worth a nominal charge to include building-code upgrade coverage, especially if the home is more than twenty years old. Insurance companies often have cost reductions for home owners who have installed a dead-bolt lock, a burglar or fire alarm, fire extinguishers, a fire-resistant roof, who are nonsmokers, or who have a fire protection system such as sprinklers. Check with your insurance agent to see if any might apply to you.

When you insure your home, you should also have a set amount for replacement of unscheduled personal property in case of a fire or burglary. This amount should provide more than enough coverage. If you need to have a larger amount set aside for this purpose than the policy states, the agent can increase the limit for a small increase in cost.

If the home's contents include jewelry, furs, china/flatware, firearms, antique furniture, fine art, a stamp or coin collection, or a computer worth more than the policy limits, it will be necessary to have a rider or a separate Valuable Items Policy. Make sure the policy has an escalator clause that will take inflation into account. It will be necessary to have the items appraised by a professional, which adds cost but is well worth it. As a matter of fact, it would be a good idea to walk around the house recording all of the possessions on videotape with commentary, and place the tape, along with receipts for all of the family's expensive purchases and a copy of the appraisal, in a safe-deposit box at a local bank. It would also be a good idea to place valuables such as jewelry, coins, or a stamp collection in the box too, for safekeeping.

Insurance policies are available that provide all-risk coverage (theft, fire, earthquake, flood, and even accidental breakage) for treasured collectibles at the full stated value. Blanket coverage will protect the entire collection up to a stated maximum value per item, up to a defined total. Additional blanket coverage can be purchased as well as increased coverage on specific items. Like the Valuable Items Policy, a home owner should have the collection appraised and videotaped. Also, check to see whether an inflation-guard feature automatically increases the value of scheduled items. A partial list of items that can be insured in a collectible insurance policy includes: figurines, dolls, teddy bears, toys, model cars, music boxes, miniatures, collector plates, ornaments, animation art, sports memorabilia (other than cards), and model railroads.

As a guideline, a personal-liability home owner's policy for $300,000, which includes injury and property damage for each occurrence and aggregate personal injury, is sufficient. Employer liability of $100,000 will cover domestic labor and a baby-sitter. If you have a live-in caregiver or nanny, check to see whether additional liability is needed. Unless a residence is used for a home business, you will not need coverage for workers' compensation, business computers, and capital equipment.

Unless your home is near an earthquake fault, it will not be necessary to have earthquake insurance, which adds approximately 50 percent to the premium. It would be wise, though, to check for any strong earth movements in your area in the past prior to buying coverage.

For people living in or along a flood plain, it would be a good idea to purchase a policy underwritten by the Federal National Flood Insurance Program. Again, the premium is high compared to what is covered, but this is just about the only protection in case of flooding. Other natural perils are often not covered at all. For example, if a landslide should topple a home from the crest of a hill, few policies would offer protection. If the same house should slide, causing a gas main to rupture resulting in an explosion or fire, the house would be covered only under the fire protection provisions of the home owner's policy. In case of a mudslide resulting in water damage, a home owner may not have recourse for filing a loss. Water damage normally is only covered in case of a leaking roof, a leaking pipe, or fire-fighting. What is covered and what is not can be tricky issues so make sure you spend time with the agent going over what is relevant for your home and area.

Many high-net-worth households find living in an average neighborhood away from any flood plains or fault lines suits them best. By necessity, high income–low net worth families have higher insurance expenses because they buy larger, higher-priced homes that are more costly to insure.

One home owner who found having a policy to protect against unforeseen loss a necessity was Ashley R., an investment banker. Ashley believed she had a water leak in the kitchen wall of her twenty-two-year-old home. The leak had been caused by hot and cold water pipes crossing over and touching one another during the construction of the house. Electrolysis slowly ate away at the hot water pipe. After paying a manageable deductible of $500 on her home owner's insurance, Ashley learned that the insurance company spent more than $11,400 for the full repairs.

If the home owner's insurance is the first line of protection for a home, automobile insurance is the front line of defense for the family's vehicles and personal liability exposure. As with expensive homes, new luxury cars cost more to insure.

Some automobile insurance carriers specialize in servicing certain groups, such as government workers or educators. There are also companies that underwrite policies directly with drivers who have good records. Firms also offer good driver discounts, good student discounts, multi-car discounts, and anti-theft device discounts. There are also rate reductions for people older than fifty-five who qualify for a mature driver program. Some companies also offer reduced rates for automobiles with air bags and anti-lock brakes.

Again, as with home owner's insurance, don't only consider the lowest cost provider. Keep in mind the following issues: the number of claims the company processes per year; their responsiveness in paying out claims; whether they will allow a consumer to take a car to a repair shop of their own choice; how difficult and expensive it will be to place a youthful driver on the policy; whether they require repair shops to use only after-market parts rather than original equipment parts; and how rates may change if a claim is filed.

A number of states have recently passed laws requiring proof of insurance. For the most part, a high-net-worth household should have more than the minimum required coverage for the state in which they reside. The following is a rough guideline: $100,000 for bodily injury to each person, $300,000 for each accident; $100,000 for property damage for each accident; $30,000 uninsured motorist coverage for each person; and $60,000 for each accident. Comprehensive (fire and theft) and collision insurance (damage to your car) are based on the automobile's actual cash value less the deductible. If you are willing to risk a higher deductible, you can lower the premium. It seems reasonable to keep a deductible of $200–$500. At some point collision insurance will be too costly compared to the car's value. Insurance agents suggest multiplying the cost of the premium for collision insurance by 10. If that number is higher than the actual cash value of the car, then drop the coverage. Eliminating collision coverage makes sense for older cars, especially since you save enough money to fix the damage or buy another pre-owned car. It would also be a good idea to include rental reimbursement in a policy in case your car is in the repair shop for a while due to a collision. Consider waiving the deductible for uninsured motorists because it is so inexpensive.

Many high-net-worth families obtain automobile roadside assistance through a car manufacturer or an automobile cooperative. This service will take care of jump-starting a car, changing tires, and local towing charges. It may be worthwhile to have long-distance towing included in the automobile policy.

Should the family own an extra car that it uses sparingly, it is possible to reduce the insurance so long as the car is not intended for business or commuting use. Usually, the coverage limits the car to 2,500–3,500 miles annually and it then becomes a pleasure vehicle.

Collectible automobiles can be insured for less than vehicles technically used for pleasure, but the terms are far more stringent. Because high-net-worth households keep their cars for such a long time, many of the automobiles become collectibles. In addition, a number of high-net-worth households have kept automobiles from their youth or bought a car to restore for reasons of nostalgia. A collectible, after restoration to better-than-showroom condition, is often taken to car club events, car shows, or used in parades. A vehicle of this nature can also be taken on occasional drives to keep the bearings lubricated, so long as the total use is kept under 2,500 miles per year. Recently, some carriers are making a 5,000-mile option available for an added fee. In either case, however, the car cannot be used for general transportation. The automobile insurer does not intend this type of vehicle to be used as a family car or as a back-up to the family automobile.

Buying a Personal Excess Liability Policy (often called an Umbrella Policy) is wise when a family has a net worth approaching $250,000. This type of insurance extends coverage of $1 million for personal liability for each occurrence. The household's automobiles and primary residence are automatically protected under the provisions of this policy. Because of the litigious nature of American society, it is absolutely essential that high-net-worth households buy this safeguard. It is an extension of the automobile policy and in order to purchase and retain this type of protection, the primary auto insurance must be in force for all exposures for at least the following automobile liability limits: bodily injury $100,000 each person and $300,000 each occurrence; property damage $50,000 each occurrence; and bodily injury and property damage combined (comprehensive personal liability) $100,000 each occurrence. If the family owns rental property, motorcycles, recreational vehicles, or has a youthful operator driving a motor vehicle, additional charges will apply. As an affluent family increases its net worth past $1 million, it can increase its personal liability in increments from $2 million to $5 million.

A policy for boats and yachts and a separate policy for recreational vehicles (RVs) and motorcycles are necessary for households owning these types of craft and conveyances. With automobile and specialized insurance, here, too, high income–low net worth households tend to pay a lot more in premiums because they purchase new luxury makes of watercraft and RVs.

People who own their own business need to either self-insure or purchase company protection and those who work for others should look into the following protection from their employers: individual or group health insurance; disability insurance; and term, universal, or variable life insurance, depending upon circumstances. For the high net worth, life insurance is a very important estate-planning tool. As of 1999, the IRS provides that a husband and wife can leave their family or heirs up to $1.3 million ($650,000 each) after their deaths without the recipients having to pay estate or gift taxes. Estate taxes, which can be as much as 55 percent, will be levied on any amount above this. Life insurance can be purchased to pay the estate taxes above the $1.3 million level (or $650,000 for an individual) at the time of the parents' death.

BANKERS

In the past twenty years, banking has changed dramatically. People used to identify with a particular bank and did not move their money around a great deal. As banking has become more of a commodity, consumers have learned to shop for the bank charging the lowest fees on its services. The high net worth might contract with a different bank for each service. For example, they might use one bank for a safe-deposit box, another for a checking account, and a third for a credit card. High-net-worth households aren't shy about negotiating these fees downward in return for their business.

High-net-worth entrepreneurs need a banker for a reason that a high-net-worth corporate employee does not—for business loans. It is a fact that most large banks do not want to deal with small businesses. They focus, instead, on medium- and large-sized companies. Should they entertain the idea of making a small loan, the matter is usually delegated to a junior lending officer where inexperience and turnover can be a problem.

The best way to find a banker is to obtain recommendations from other entrepreneurs or small businesses in the area. After you gather at least three names, stop by and introduce yourself. It is vital to learn more about the banks that you are investigating. Tell them that you are looking for a relationship, but do not settle for the first "yes" that you hear. The following questions will help guide you:

1. Learn whether the bank has an industry specialty. This area will give an idea of how the bank might serve the loan needs of your enterprise.

2. Ask about the bank's loan-to-deposit ratio. Banks are required to publish this ratio in the local newspaper four times a year. If the ratio is below 50 percent, this means the bank is too cautious about lending money.

3. Ask about the bank's capital ratio. This is the ratio of capital to assets. This indicator measures the bank's strength and its capital availability. The ratio should exceed 6 percent. Below this level the bank may be having difficulties.

4. Inquire about the banker's personal non-committee loan limit. This is the amount of money the banker can approve without having to go to a committee to gain loan approval. If the amount you need is very high, the committee may be unavoidable.

5. Ask how much capital the bank has. Some states allow a single customer to borrow from 15 to 20 percent of its capital. For a small bank, this may mean less than $100,000. Even if the amount is enough now, will it be enough to meet your company's future needs?

6. Obtain a list of client references, preferably owners of small businesses who can relate to your needs and concerns. Learn what other businesspeople think about the banker and the bank.

For its part, the bank will be interested in your personal character, your company's credit history, the collateral available to back the loan, personal and business cash flow, and the amount of liquid assets available.

A bank will also want to see business and personal tax returns for the last three years, a three-to-five-year financial plan, a break-even analysis if it is a start-up, a

detailed marketing plan including top clients or customers, letters of intent to purchase from prospective
clients or customers for a start-up, and information on
the competition.

Also include in the proposal the articles of incorpo-
ration, bylaws, corporate resolutions or partnership
agreements, resumes on yourself (and partners, if there
are any), letters of recommendation, copies of property
titles, proof of life insurance, and a financial disclosure
giving your net worth with copies of all current bank
and brokerage account statements.

A bank provides an essential service for the high net
worth: the safe-deposit box. It is an important place to
store valuable papers such as house records, insurance
policies, appraisals, receipts for expensive purchases,
automobile registrations, birth certificates, and pass-
ports. Valuable jewelry, stamp and coin collections
should also be locked away rather than kept at home.
Your will should be safeguarded in a fireproof vault. A
list of all individual and joint investments including:
IRAs, Keogh accounts or 401(k)s, mutual fund accounts,
money market accounts, individual stock accounts, pension plans, annuities and bank accounts should also be
placed in a guarded location. This list should include
names, addresses, and phone numbers of the pension
fund managers and all account administrators. Include
how to get in touch with your attorney, CPA or PA,
stockbroker, certified financial planner, chartered financial analyst, registered investment advisor, and insurance
agents. If something happens to one of the breadwinners,
this information will be invaluable.

Most people do not have the time to keep abreast of the changing financial landscape. A well-assembled financial team will use their expertise and knowledge to assist in either building wealth or protecting it. It is well worth the expense.

SIGNPOSTS

THE TRAVELING TEAM
Few people have the knowledge and expertise to go it alone in investing.

1. Stockbrokers assist clients to determine long-range financial goals and time frame. They can help determine the level of risk appropriate for their clients; determine and recommend stock and mutual funds; choose among new investments those that are right for the investor; and handle setting up investment accounts, IRAs, and the purchase of individual stock and mutual funds. They are paid on a commission basis, which can be a conflict of interest. The high net worth who are savvy and sophisticated in financial dealings are better suited to working with a stockbroker alone. Most members of the high net worth use a stockbroker as a watchful eye on the market, to keep track of the investor's portfolio on an everyday basis, and to offer their professional opinion.

2. A good move is to hire a fee-only advisor (fees are based on a percentage of assets under management, or time) who may be a money manager, financial planner, or both. The advisor could be either a certified financial planner, chartered financial analyst, or a registered investment advisor.

a. Use your network to find and interview at least three to five candidates.

b. Before hiring any professionals, make sure they are compatible with your personality, risk tolerance, and financial goals.

c. If you hire a certified financial planner who is also an insurance agent, be careful. You may find yourself investing in insurance products with high commissions.

d. Ensure that the advisor is registered with either the Securities and Exchange Commission, your home state's securities department, or the National Association of Securities Dealers. Also, check whether there have been any complaints lodged against the firm or advisor.

e. Check three to five references for each candidate.

3. There are more similarities than differences among the three types of investment advisors. Find a person (rather than a credential or degree) who fits your personality, investment philosophy, risk tolerance, and long-range goals.

a. A Chartered Financial Analyst (CFA) endures a rigorous three-year program that is more comprehensive and difficult than the certified financial planner's course of study. They are well qualified to set up a comprehensive plan, though they may be conservative in their financial investing. They are more apt to favor conventional instruments than new issues. Investors who prefer less risk work well with them.

b. A Certified Financial Planner (CFP) is registered with the Securities and Exchange Commission (SEC) so they can recommend as well as purchase stocks or mutual funds. They, too, can profile an investor's financial situation and goals. Also, they can develop and implement a comprehensive financial plan. CFPs can be stockbrokers, mutual fund salespeople, or insurance agents.

c. A Registered Investment Advisor (RIA) is registered with the SEC and the state securities department, as are CFAs and CFPs. They perform the same thorough review and strategic planning as the others.

d. Check out fee-only money managers or financial planners who have RIA, CFA, or CFP designations. These financial professionals can make investment decisions for clients based on their risk tolerance and goals. Fee-only financial planners, in addition, can assist investors with budgeting, taxes, life insurance, real estate, retirement, and estate planning.

4. In order to find the right certified financial planner, chartered financial analyst, or registered investment advisor you need to ask the right questions.

5. Certified Public Accountant/Public Accountant. They

are critical in preparing tax forms and helping lower exposure to business as well as individual taxes. They can also help put together financial plans and strategies, foresee and solve existing problems, offer second opinions, and refer clients to other professionals on an as-needed basis.

6. Tax Attorney. A tax attorney is helpful for medium and large businesses with complex needs. They can also devise intricate investment strategies for the high net worth. Some lawyers who specialize in taxes have established a financial planning practice by accumulating a number of financial licenses and certifications to become a one-stop shop.

7. Insurance Agents. If you want to build wealth, you cannot do it with insurance products. Insurance is best used to protect wealth. The high net worth need to have insurance against lawsuits, fires, and thefts. Service, payment of claims, and the coverage offered are as important as cost when determining the right policy.

a. Home owner's insurance protects the structure and its contents, not the land. Insure for the cost of rebuilding from the ground up. Make sure that the policy has inflation provisions for materials and workmanship.

b. A Valuable Items Policy is for replacement of costly items outside the terms of the home owner's insurance policy. Make sure you have an inflation-guard feature that automatically increases the value of scheduled items.

c. A special policy for treasured collectibles can provide all-risk coverage (theft, fire, earthquake, flood, accidental breakage) up to a full, stated value. Make sure you have an inflation-guard feature.

d. If you have a home-based business you may need a policy to provide for workers' compensation and protection of capital equipment.

e. Automobile insurance is for the protection of the family's cars. Take out the maximum insurance you can. Liability, comprehensive, collision, uninsured, and underinsured insurance should be purchased. Drop the collision provisions on a car when its yearly cost is greater than 10 percent of the actual cash value of the car. If you drive less than 3,500 miles per year, you might be able to insure the car as a pleasure vehicle. A collectible or antique automobile cannot be used as everyday transportation and still qualify for inexpensive collector-car insurance.

f. Personal Excess Liability Policy (Umbrella Policy) is important for a family having a net worth more than $250,000. This coverage extends protection on your cars and home for personal liability up to $1 million. The primary automobile insurance policy must be kept up-to-date at all times. If you have a youthful operator in the household, recreational vehicles, watercraft, motorcycles, or rental property, you will need to pay an additional charge. Additional personal liability can be purchased from $2 million to $5 million, as a family accumulates more net worth.

g. Entrepreneurs and those who work for others should have individual or group life insurance, disability insurance, and term, universal, or variable life insurance, depending on circumstances.

8. Bankers. High-net-worth entrepreneurs need to ask questions and interview bankers for the possibility of setting up business loans.

a. The high net worth use a safe-deposit box to store valuables. In addition, a videotape of the contents of the household, receipts for expensive purchases, important papers, a list of all individual and joint investments, and the legal will should be placed in this box.

b. High-net-worth families, in their search for a good value, usually deal with different banks for a safe-deposit box, a checking account, and a bank credit card.

8

A SENSE OF COMMUNITY

HIGH-NET-WORTH HOUSEHOLDS GIVE THEIR
time, expertise, and money in support of charitable and
community organizations. This sense of connecting with
the community stems from their own experiences in
childhood and adolescence. Their parents may have
been involved in community service in some form, and
they, as children, picked it up and incorporated it into
their own life. In asking why they continue to do it,
many say that they get pleasure from helping others.
They have learned people cannot find happiness by
searching for it, because happiness is found in serving
others. The high net worth who don't learn this lesson
early pick it up later in life. Their sense of community
extends from the family to the neighborhood and out to
the larger society.

The high net worth provide a secure, rooted, loving

environment for their family. They tend to have a good relationship with their extended family. They host important family gatherings at their home to reinforce traditions and customs with their kin. The high net worth resolve to do things as a family: go skating or sledding, read together, play a game, attend events, go out to dinner, attend services, etc. They participate with their children in youth development and charitable activities.

Once a business has been established or a profession mastered, it is very easy to fall into complacency. Without new goals or a new direction to aim for, the same activities day in and day out become boring. In addition to finding a new meaning in their business endeavors, the high net worth discover a new vitality by helping others. The high net worth believe that when one gives or shares without thought of personal benefit, the reward will return manyfold.

The corporate high net worth recognize the benefit of fine-tuning and enhancing their management skills within an organization in the service of others. The entrepreneurial high net worth understand that a lack of social responsibility may make their firm more liable to fines and lawsuits. More importantly, positive community relations enhance the company's reputation. As a concerned employer, it can attract and retain employees and position itself as a supplier of choice.

CHARITABLE ORGANIZATIONS

The high income–low net worth display a common thread in their reasoning for providing donations to charity: they see a tax write-off on the federal tax form. It is certainly a noble gesture to provide cash gifts to nonprofit organizations, but the fixation on tax savings is misdirected. A tax break is not the same as saving money. The taxpayer is only able to obtain small relief—cents on the dollar—based on their tax bracket.

The high income–low net worth often use charitable events as a way to attain social and economic prominence in the community, so they favor conservative, middle-of-the-road causes.

This is less true of the high net worth. Should a family member suffer a tragedy, no matter what form, there is a strong possibility the high-net-worth family will take an active part in the organization without worrying about social approval from the community at large.

Marion I., an executive in the airline industry, had a child with developmental disabilities. Thirty years ago, society institutionalized juveniles and adults in wards at state mental hospitals or in separate facilities for the mentally retarded. In the 1970s, Marion supported state legislation to set up extensive training for people with developmental disabilities and to establish halfway houses where they could live together. Marion, along with others, helped spearhead the change in how society treated the developmentally disabled and helped close a sad and tragic chapter in mental health care in her state.

Some CEOs hire publicists to advertise their organization's good work. Gary W., a president of a Fortune 500 consumer products subsidiary, uses highly visible community outreach programs to advance his company as one of the corporate leaders in the region. This publicity helps everyone concerned with the project.

The low net worth usually give money to charity on an ongoing basis through their work (the United Way is an example), but they do not have a sizeable estate. In contrast, the high net worth frequently grant money from their estate to a favorite cause. The immensely wealthy have the resources to set up foundations, large trusts, or endowments (funds or property) for the benefit of non-profit organizations.

A 1999 survey by the United States Trust Company reveals why wealthy Americans give. It interviewed the top 1 percent of wealthy Americans, those with a new worth in excess of $3 million. Ninety-seven percent of this group actively participated in charitable giving at an average of 8 percent of their after-tax income. This statistic contradicts the general opinion that the affluent are not as generous as average Americans. When asked what motivated them to donate, 79 percent said they gave because of a desire to support worthwhile causes. Sixty-nine percent said they believe the financially successful have a responsibility to share their good fortune. The high net worth act as if giving is a moral investment to be made.

The high net worth also know money is only one scarce resource they can allocate. They understand that time and energy are just as vital—if not more so—to an organization's survival. Many take a leading role in a non-profit organization or lend their particular expertise on an ongoing basis. The United States Trust Company survey found that the high net worth volunteer an average of seventeen hours per month to charities they support, with religious organizations and educational institutions receiving the most support.

Erin H., a chief operating officer of a hospital, had a child with a hereditary disease. She got involved in the local chapter of a nonprofit organization devoted to the course of the disease and its treatment. Although she was not aspiring to effect policy changes, as the above-mentioned Marion did, she knew that whatever time she could give would be important to the organization. As a volunteer, she helped out with direct mailings, local education programs, and a once-a-year fundraiser.

EDUCATION

High-net-worth corporate executives and entrepreneurs often get involved in high-school programs for disadvantaged or troubled youngsters. They enjoy discussing with students the value of education, hard work, perseverance, and discipline, and their own stories of personal success can make a lasting impression. Many entrepreneurs have also provided internships and work-study opportunities for high-school students. In some instances, students who have shown a strong work ethic have eventually been hired by those companies.

High-net-worth entrepreneurs who have not completed college are often tempted to return to school to complete their degree requirements and gain knowledge that will help them run their business better. The high income–low net worth often pursue degree and certificate programs as well, but they fear losing their jobs if they don't stay current.

The corporate high net worth have other reasons to pursue more education. They are more likely to return to school for an MBA or pursue a degree in a different field for an impending career change. Jay V., a senior manager for a national day care organization with a B.A. degree in hand, returned to school in his early forties in order to acquire an executive MBA. Jay was interested in changing careers and hoped the advanced business training would help him better compete in the job market with other senior executives. After acquiring his degree, he received an offer from a high-tech company for a position in south Florida at the corporate headquarters.

Many high income–low net worth households donate to the college or university they attended, particularly if their employer matches their gift up to a specific dollar amount. The high income–low net worth are also more likely to give donations, outside of matching programs, to their choice of college while they are still living.

High-net-worth entrepreneurs are more likely to give their time and experience to their alma mater than to donate large cash gifts, unless they have many millions of dollars in net worth. In that case, endowments might be made, class buildings constructed, academic chairs dedicated in their names, and they might be invited to become a member of the board of trustees. Despite the interest of the college development office in receiving money early, both the corporate and entrepreneurial high net worth give money at their discretion, usually at the death of both spouses. The amount is usually given as a scholarship in the name of the benefactors. An alternative is to give the money in trust to the college which, in turn, dispenses the money to students who can demonstrate financial need and show academic promise.

A favorite endeavor for high-net-worth entrepreneurs is to lecture at local universities. Colleges seek business leaders with strong hands-on work experience, and they have found the high net worth can be exceptional in the classroom. Some have thus put their advanced degrees to good use by teaching at the high school, community college, or university level.

John K., a director of operations in a high-tech electronics firm, finished his Ph.D. in business at a local university and accepted a position as an assistant professor at a leading university on the West Coast. At the same time, he began consulting on a part-time basis with local firms and even took a position for a few hours a week as vice president of administration for a start-up computer peripherals firm. With his advanced degree, John was able to create a varied job schedule for himself that appealed to his interests in both teaching and the corporate world.

COMMUNITY ASSOCIATIONS

The high net worth have an inclination to seek out leadership positions in community and civic organizations. After being successful in business, they want to carry this over into neighborhood associations and the larger community. They like to have a say in how things are being run, especially if they believe there is room for improvement. What irks them most are the people on the sidelines pleading for different results but not willing to get involved themselves.

Corporations and large companies prefer their employees become involved in a variety of community projects. It gives the company visibility and expands the employees' professional and personal development. Employees also gain contacts that could result in future clients. For others, it is a way to spend time away from the daily grind of familiar work. For entrepreneurial firms, community service is a way to be an active member in the community and a continuing presence.

For example, Clare S., who owned a number of office buildings offering executive suite space to small businesses, contacted the city's Chamber of Commerce to inquire how he might become involved in community service. The executive director of the Chamber told Clare that the city council was creating a team of business people to assist in retaining and attracting new business. Clare was asked to co-chair one of the six business teams. Inspired by the thought of working with a number of business leaders for a common cause, he agreed. In the first year of his service, Clare's team assisted in successfully negotiating to retain a subsidiary of a Fortune 500 company in the food service industry.

As another example, Pamela R., a financial officer for an after-market automobile parts firm, decided to assist the local military base's efforts to help needy children at Christmas. She began a corporate "Toys for Tots" program in her community. If a business could not drop off toys at the air force base, they could leave wrapped toys at her place of work, where she would collect and deliver them herself using the firm's truck. If the company contacts were too far away, she would direct the firm's truck to pick up the toys. This program has been successful for many years now. Not only has it benefited low-income families and homeless children, but Pamela's company has received numerous write-ups in the local press that have been good for business.

PROFESSIONAL AFFILIATIONS

Successful business people enjoy working with other professionals in their field who share their same concerns. Corporate executives and entrepreneurs use professional organizations as an open forum to discuss business trends, rally support for issues affecting their industry, and lobby for change.

Nadine B., an owner of a temporary services firm, joined a professional organization in her field. She quickly found an opportunity to help the organization lobby against the state legislature passing a restrictive new law. The state was considering a bill imposing a $10,000 bond on all professional employees in organizations engaged in outplacement. The professional organization, in league with outplacement firms that had established their own professional association, lobbied heavily and scotched the state's attempt for new legislation. In her second year in the association, Nadine became a member of the speakers committee, and began looking for monthly speakers who could talk with authority about future trends in the industry. She worked not only for the benefit of the organization, but also for herself, since she, too, learned a lot about her field from these speakers.

Stan A., a human resources director for a company in the entertainment field, joined a local chapter of a nationwide professional human resources organization. He wanted to meet others in the human resources community and learn how they dealt with problems. As a further benefit, Stan was able to watch and learn how his colleagues recruited new talent.

In addition, the association set up a job hot line where Stan could explore new positions that became available. This professional organization provided a network for Stan to make contacts within his field's hidden job market, where it is said more than 80 percent of jobs are found.

Leadership can also be displayed in assisting those struggling new entrants into the field, recent college graduates, and people changing careers. Through example, instruction and training, and by the setting of high professional standards of excellence, many of the high net worth who have been in a career a long time find a new vitality in their industry. The high net worth also find that by sharing their vision of where they believe the industry is going, they can help others prepare for future change. Instead of being resistant to new efforts, many of the high-net-worth leaders are attempting to effect change-readiness and hardiness in their employees and others, as they witness their industry continuing to go through turbulence.

The high income–low net worth who get involved in professional organizations generally do so to gain standing in their profession, for contacts in case of a job loss, or to look for other opportunities. Much of their energy and drive is to maintain their current status rather than to innovate or create. The continual struggle to keep a high-income stream intact saps much of their vitality. The need to remain at their current standard of living is a source of worry.

The corporate high-net-worth exhibit less anxiety since they have a deeper financial base from which to draw should they lose their job. They usually have good networking contacts and an inordinate amount of time to find the right situation. The entrepreneurial high net worth may worry about their business, but they feel in complete control of their destiny. If their business should fold, they would look for other opportunities to master. A high-net-worth person who loses a business or a fortune can pick up the pieces and rebuild. Many entrepreneurs have done this several times. Even in the midst of failed business ventures, they remain more independent than the high income–low net worth group.

The $1 million-net-worth family has invested wisely to get where they are. After becoming financially independent, a high-net-worth couple can devote more of their time to interests outside of business. Involvement in charities, community work, and professional associations gives them great pleasure and satisfaction.

SIGNPOSTS

A SENSE OF COMMUNITY
High-net-worth households support charity, education and community organizations, and professional associations.

1. ONCE A BUSINESS IS WELL ESTABLISHED, THE HIGH NET WORTH NEED NEW CHALLENGES. THEY HAVE MORE TIME FOR CREATING, HELPING OTHERS, AND FINDING NEW INTERESTS.

2. THE HIGH INCOME–LOW NET WORTH USE GIFT-GIVING MAINLY AS A TAX WRITE-OFF.

3. CHARITIES ARE USED BY THE HIGH NET WORTH AS A RALLYING POINT FOR PUBLIC SUPPORT ON CONTROVERSIAL CAUSES.

a. The high net worth give their time and energy for causes they believe in.

b. Frequently, they leave money for charities in their wills.

4. CORPORATE AND ENTREPRENEURIAL HIGH-NET-WORTH FAMILIES GET INVOLVED IN EDUCATION.

a. They may volunteer time in high school programs for youngsters with disadvantaged or troubled backgrounds.

b. High-net-worth entrepreneurial parents who have not completed college often return to finish it, and those that have often pursue advanced degrees.

c. The high net worth often give their time and experience to their alma maters.

d. The extremely wealthy endow colleges.

e. Many of the high net worth leave money to colleges in their legal wills, mostly in the form of scholarships.

5. THE HIGH NET WORTH SEEK OUT LEADERSHIP POSITIONS IN COMMUNITY AND CIVIC ORGANIZATIONS.

a. They want to give back to the community.

b. They enjoy being involved with other business leaders.

6. ANOTHER PRIME AREA FOR INVOLVEMENT IS PROFESSIONAL AFFILIATIONS.

a. They can share concerns, issues, and problems.

b. They also use the organization to lobby for change or maintain the status quo.

9

RETIREMENT

FOR GENERATIONS MOST AMERICANS EQUATED retirement with leaving work and enjoying an extended vacation. Very few people nowadays view sitting in a rocking chair, watching television, and occasionally snacking as a satisfying way to pass the time.

About 50 percent of the people who stop working at age sixty-five are relatively satisfied. Another 25 percent quickly become disillusioned with retirement and many return to work within two years. The remaining 25 percent are people who are simply unable to work, primarily for health reasons.

Today, 12 percent of people over sixty-five are still in the workforce. This will drastically change as the oldest baby boomers begin reaching their mid-sixties by the year 2011. Financial experts are predicting that more and more older couples will be unable to retire fully. Statistics provided by the U.S. Census Bureau demonstrate this sad fact. Nearly 70 percent of Americans age sixty-five and over find themselves with a household income of less than $25,000 per year. Almost 45 percent of Americans in this group have household incomes of less than $15,000 per year, just over the poverty line for a family of four. By the year 2005, around 54 percent of retirees will be in serious economic difficulty. Many of these people may have had sizeable incomes at one time but rather meager nest eggs. Their failure to plan for their financial future during their working years will come back to haunt them.

Social Security has been an important portion of retirement funds for millions of American families for more than sixty years. Intended as a supplement, it is historically supposed to account for 20–30 percent of the average, middle-income worker's retirement. In reality, however, it might be closer to 60 or 70 percent for low-net-worth households.

SOCIAL SECURITY

Social Security, as it was originally conceived in 1935, was designed as a pay-as-you-go program. Established to assist survivors, the disabled, the unemployed, and the retired, it was supposed to fill a vacuum where no protection previously existed. As initially established, the Old-Age, Survivors, and Disability Insurance (OASDI) meant that a worker's payroll tax deductions were not set aside for their benefit when they retired; instead, they were used to pay for the benefits of those who were already retired.

The case of the first Social Security recipient, Ida May Fuller, gives a glimpse of how the system is structured. Social Security Administration records show that in May 1940 Fuller had paid a grand total of $24.75 in payroll taxes from 1937 through 1939. Her monthly benefit check began at $22.54 and, because she lived to be one hundred years of age, she ultimately collected $22,888 from the system—$924 in benefits collected for each $1 in taxes paid. But Fuller was the exception.

At the start of Social Security, the average American's life expectancy was just sixty-two, and the over-sixty-five population was small. Since then, life expectancy has climbed to seventy-nine for females and seventy-three for males, which means being on Social Security for two or three decades is no longer the exception. To keep up, Congress has frequently increased the payroll tax rate and the wage base on which it was levied.

Although the United States population is aging, it is not growing old as fast as those of most other industrial countries. It is predicted that by the year 2030 America's sixty-five-and-older population will be 20 percent of its total, up from 12 percent now. One explanation for the United States turning gray relatively slowly is that its birthrate is high, compared to industrial nations' standards. The United States rate is 2.1 live births per woman, enough to keep the population growing at a modest rate.

In January 1999, the National Academy on an Aging Society issued a report stating that the "management dependency ratio," referring to the relative numbers of people too young or too old to work who must be supported by the working-age population, is more favorable than two or three decades ago. The report mentioned that the dependency problem was worse in the 1960s and 1970s—when masses of baby boomers were children and adolescents—than it will be in the next forty years, when baby boomers will stop working. Because the proportion of children will be relatively low, the study concluded that the nation will be able to shift resources from the young to the old without having to expend a greater share of the nation's wealth to service the retired. In 1960 there were ninety people of dependent age (ages zero to nineteen, and sixty-five and older) for every one hundred workers between the ages of twenty and sixty-four. Even in the year 2040, when the elderly's share of the population will be far greater than it is now, there will be only seventy-nine persons of dependent age for every one hundred working-age Americans.

Other experts warn that Social Security has become less of a windfall for each succeeding generation. Workers with average earnings who retired in 1975 needed just two years of benefits to recapture all the money they had paid into Social Security. Workers who retired in 1997 needed nine years and eight months of benefits to break even, and those who are forty-nine years old and still working as of 1999 will need seventeen years of benefits.

Although surpluses are expected to continue building until the year 2012, the Social Security system eventually is going to run a deficit when the oldest of the baby boomers reach retirement age. Over the next three decades, the number of program participants will rise from 39 million to 70 million people. Where there are now 3.4 workers paying Medicare and Social Security taxes for every retiree, it is estimated the ratio will be only 2.1 workers paying for every beneficiary in 2030. A critical event of major proportions is brewing. The issue of Social Security may be remembered as the last problem of the twentieth century or the first crisis of the twenty-first.

Most financial experts project that Medicare's hospital trust fund will go bankrupt in the year 2015 and Social Security will be unable to pay all of its promised benefits in 2034. At this point, the Social Security program will exhaust the surplus now accumulating (and being spent on other government programs), and annual payroll taxes will only be able to provide 75 percent of benefits.

There are four possible long-term solutions to the dilemma: 1) Make people work longer before they can tap fully into the system; 2) allow workers to place at least part of their money into private stock and bond accounts and earn greater returns; 3) increase payroll tax payments and expand the wage base from its current level set by law; or 4) use the growing surplus in the federal budget to fund the system through a partial privatization program and a new type of private retirement account.

With regard to the first solution, the American government can clearly make people work longer before allowing them to receive retirement benefits. A 1983 law pushed the age of qualification for full benefits to age sixty-six for those born in 1943 and age sixty-seven for those born in 1960 and later. Boosting the age for full Social Security benefits to age seventy has become a component of many congressional proposals for saving the program. So far, there is very little support among the American people for increasing the age again.

As for the second solution, Social Security, as a pay-as-you-go system, means taxes paid by 138 million workers are transferred to the 43 million beneficiaries collecting payments as retirees, the disabled, and their survivors. To increase the amount of money in the system, a growing number of elected officials and non-governmental experts want the current system altered so that each worker's deductions would be set aside for that worker's retirement.

The thinking is that the "individual account" could be invested by the government or individual worker. These investments would have the potential to bring about greater returns—with obviously greater risks—than the U.S. securities in which today's Social Security surplus must be invested. Privatizers point to the small investment return Social Security recipients receive compared to potentially huge returns on Wall Street. Financial experts contend that Wall Street stands to gain 100 million new accounts if the system is either privatized or semi-privatized, and could earn billions of dollars in fees.

Detractors of privatization believe there would be too much reliance on a widely fluctuating market. Although governments have learned how to navigate around economic disasters since the Great Depression, not every investor makes prudent investment decisions.

Privatization is already gaining a head of steam in another part of the world. In 1999, Poland began gradually instituting partial privatization. Poland faces the same problem encountered by many countries: With the proportion of elderly to workers expected to rise rapidly in the early years of the next century, payments to pensioners will increase far beyond the system's revenue stream. Poland is shifting toward an arrangement where all workers depend on privately managed investment funds for more than a third of their retirement benefits. Since middle-aged Polish workers have limited investing years left, the government decided that those less than thirty years old as of January 1, 1999, are required to join the new system, while those fifty or older are not eligible. People in the thirty to forty-nine age range must choose in late 1999 whether to remain entirely in the state-run system or shift part of the contributions to a private fund.

The Polish privatization program will shift 37.5 percent of workers' and employers' contributions to privately managed pension funds that will invest in stocks and bonds. The government also aims to strengthen the country's economic growth by boosting rates of saving and investing. Government plans call for gradually increasing the proportion of contributions invested privately to 50 percent. The Polish government also hopes the system will encourage more private investment.

The third alternative—increasing the payroll tax and wage base—also has merit. Rather than pay the current 6.2 percent rate, workers would contribute 7.3 percent of their wages to Social Security in order to change the system from pay-as-you-go to workers paying for their own retirement. For the self-employed, the rate would increase from 12.4 percent to 14.6 percent. In addition, if the income cap on payroll tax was hiked from the current

$68,000 to $97,000 per year, the problem would be moved to the year 2073. No one has polled the American public to determine whether they would be willing to pay 1 percent more in payroll taxes to keep the system solvent. Fearing a backlash from voters, Congress has decided not to touch this politically charged approach.

Concerning the fourth possible solution to the Social Security dilemma, on January 19, 1999, President Clinton advanced a plan to reform the ailing Social Security system and put off its day of reckoning from the year 2034 to 2055. He asked that projected federal budget surpluses for the next fifteen years be diverted to the Social Security system. This may entail more political hope than economic reality. Historical precedent has shown it is likely the nation will face one or perhaps two economic recessions in the next fifteen years, which means that balancing the federal budget, let alone generating a surplus, may be a pipe dream. President Clinton proposes that 25 percent of the surplus be invested in the private sector in the form of stocks, bonds, and other investments. The stock market would be slightly influenced by this new infusion of cash.

As a second feature of the Clinton proposal, the president envisions that 11 percent of the future budget surpluses—estimated at $480 billion over the next fifteen years—be used to supplement traditional Social Security benefits. Clinton has seemingly adopted the Republican belief that the stock market provides a better rate of return in the long run than Treasury securities. Historically, the real return on stocks, after taking inflation into account, is close to 7 percent per year. This is in contrast to a real return of 3 percent or so on Treasury bills. This portion of the program calls for setting up and funding a separate, private retirement account for each working American called a "universal savings account" or "USA." Workers would be allowed to invest their account in stocks, bonds, or mutual funds. Under the Clinton plan, every worker would start out with the same amount from the federal government. Workers could add more of their own money to the tax-deferred accounts and the government would match their contribution up to a specified limit.

A third feature is the abolition of the "earnings test" that reduces Social Security benefits for retirees who continue to work. As current law now stands, if a person between the ages of sixty-five and sixty-nine continues to work and has earnings in 1999 of more than $15,500 (going up to $17,000 in the year 2000), $1 in benefits is withheld for every $3 above the limit. In the year 2001 the limit becomes $25,000. It increases again to $30,000 for the year 2002. After the year 2002, a formula will be devised by Congress to keep the upper limit of earnings in line with inflation.

For those under age sixty-five, the annual exempt amount is $8,640 (going up to $9,600 in the year 2000), and $1 in benefits is withheld for every $2 in earnings above the exempt amount. Each year Congress will determine and legislate any changes in the threshold limit for those under sixty-five years of age. The eligible worker who is seventy or over receives the full benefit regardless of earnings.

When thinking about the coming crisis, there are some

bright spots. High levels of immigration—900,000 new people a year—are resulting in a massive transfer of wealth to the United States. The influx of young workers arriving at the start of their productive years will help defray the pay-as-you-go retirement benefits to aging baby boomers. The median age of the immigrants has been twenty-seven for men and twenty-nine for women, so they face several decades of working and paying Social Security taxes before collecting benefits. A 1998 joint study by the Cato Institute think tank and the National Immigration Forum found that because 70 percent of immigrants are eighteen years or older, the nation has already saved $1.43 trillion by inheriting workers whose schooling was paid for by other countries. Furthermore, because only 3 percent of immigrants are over sixty-five years of age, compared to 12 percent of Americans overall, it is predicted the net benefit to the Social Security system will be nearly $150 billion by the year 2022. This amount will help offset the deficit to an extent, but it is not nearly enough to bail out Social Security.

A few authorities argue that only the truly needy should be able to receive Social Security benefits. This would not do much for reducing the Social Security deficit in the years ahead because the number of wealthy retirees is small, but it is a tempting idea that might become more popular because of the political attractiveness of using wealth-bashing as a distraction from the real problem at hand. Whether this will come to pass or not, high-networth families will be well fixed. They will have a large nest egg taking them into retirement years with confidence and prosperity.

For the average household, the Social Security controversy does not make much difference. Even figuring in Social Security benefits and pensions from companies, more than 50 percent of Americans cannot think of retiring. In 1950 almost one out of every two workers in the sixty-five-and-over group was still working; in 1960, one out of three, and in 1970, one out of five workers were still employed. The number of workers who will by necessity have to work after sixty-five is again inching up because of the lackluster savings rate. By the year 2011 it is estimated that eight out of ten will have to keep working at least part-time after they retire. A third of this group will work on a part-time basis because they enjoy it. They have enough investments and savings to tide them over for at least a portion of their retirement years. Others will try a new full-time career or start their own business. About 25 percent will have to work because they will need the money just to get by.

This suggests some very dramatic changes in the workplace. Large employers will have to invest in more training to keep their older workers up-to-date. In addition, Congress will have to consider changes in employment laws that will make it easier for older people to work longer.

On the other side of the coin, it is estimated that about five out of every one hundred baby-boomer households will have a net worth of at least $1 million by the year 2005. Another 15 percent will have enough to take them at least fifteen years into retirement—to around eighty years of age. If they live well below their means for five to ten years after they retire and leave their investments untouched, they could have enough to last into their nineties.

But without a substantial change in the way the average American household spends and invests, the baby-boom generation is not likely to do as well in retirement as the generation that grew up in the 1920s and 1930s. Besides being prodigious investors, the earlier generation lived in an era of low inflation and purchased homes at relatively low cost after World War II. This generation was also a recipient of rapidly escalating land values during the 1970s and 1980s. If they were lucky enough to have bought prime real estate in the 1950s, they might have seen their land increase in value tenfold.

The number of Americans who retire each year is pegged at nearly 2 million people, and the median age of retirement currently is sixty-two. One-third of all retirees leave the workforce by age fifty-five. The 4.1 million high-net-worth households look at retirement as a new phase of their life cycle and not necessarily as a time to stop working. A predominant number of the high net worth get pleasure and a sense of fulfillment from their work. Although corporate high-net-worth workers retire as early as their fifties, they embark on second careers. A considerable number of baby boomers have not been as fortunate.

Since the early 1980s, many companies have been hiring in growing business areas while reducing employment in less promising markets, an emerging pattern throughout the economy that helps explain why so many layoffs have come in a time of prosperity. Even though the buoyant national economy is producing lots of new jobs, this is little solace to workers worried about having to move or being forced to accept lower-paying positions. The recession of 1990 and the ongoing downsizing of American industry have cut short the careers of up to 8 million managers forced to retire as early as age fifty. A majority of these people are still not working, although they are no longer counted on the rolls of the unemployed.

DEFINED BENEFIT PLAN

Millions of Americans who have a company-defined benefit plan a pension that offers set monthly payments for life—may not know that the month they retire often affects how much they will receive. Unfortunately, there is no simple rule indicating which month is most advantageous to the retiree. In fact, the most lucrative months in which to retire vary from plan to plan and, sometimes, from year to year.

Plan participants must be careful and ask the right questions to determine which month nets the best payments. While this may take some work, it will be well worth it in the long run. Most plans multiply a percentage of one's pay by the years of service accrued. Each plan may calculate these years differently. Many plans base it on the date of hire, others on calendar or fiscal year, still others on the number of hours worked. A second timing issue is the choice of a lump-sum payment over monthly payments. Lifelong monthly payments are subject to change; a lump sum is not. The monthly payments are derived from a formula that takes into account the anticipated monthly benefit, anticipated life span of the retiree, and the current interest rates. While the monthly benefit and expected life span will not change from month to month, interest rates will. If a person plans to take a lump sum, it is important for the retiree to ask when the interest rate is adjusted. The majority of them change once a year, in January, so retirement in January may mean more money than retirement in December.

The high net worth normally elect to take the lump sum over monthly payments in order to take control of all the money due them. They expect to obtain a higher rate of return through investment than keeping the money with their former company's pension fund. This translates into making considerably more money through interest and dividends over the course of time.

Defined benefit plans that typically pay a percentage of one's salary can be tricky. The retirement month can affect which year's salary is used because some plans only count full-year salaries. Thus, if a worker retires in September, that year's salary would not count for the pension formula. If that year happened to be the highest-paid year, as it is for many retirees, it could cost the retiree thousands of dollars in lost benefits.

A retiree can take a few precautions to ensure making the best choice possible. First, obtain a copy of the plan's summary description from the plan administrator or the company's benefit representative and read it carefully. The description is a long and complex legal document, but it explains how and when benefits are calculated. Second, discuss your plan's formula with the company's benefit representative. Third, take the document to your financial advisor or planner and let them go over it as well. Have the designated member of your traveling financial team deal with the company's benefit representative to ensure the correct judgment is made on your behalf.

Jeff H., a sales executive for a company in the retail trade, turned fifty-eight on his last birthday and hoped to hang on with his company until age sixty, when he would be eligible for an early retirement package. Unfortunately, his company faced increased competition and was forced to retrench, letting go many of its department heads and executives. Although he had been with the company for more than twenty years and had strong sales figures, he was laid off with a lengthy severance of eighteen months and extended health and dental benefits to cover the same time frame. Jeff realized that he would not be entitled to early retirement and an enhanced benefit package because the severance took him just short of his sixtieth birthday. He negotiated to bridge his income (in this case severance) an additional three months, so he could retire at age sixty and receive his company's enhanced pension. The company agreed. In return, Jeff consented not to work for a competitor while he received his severance. In fact, he waited until his company pension came into force before he began to consult on a part-time basis with his former employer.

LIFE PLANNING

Generations ago retirement was viewed as a culmination of one's active, useful working life. People withdrew from the workforce at a set time and began a life of leisure. Typically, the average retiree was sixty-five years of age and the average retirement lasted maybe five or ten years at most. There was no necessity to plan, since there were few choices to make.

Richard Bolles in *The Three Boxes of Life* was one of the first authors to explore a new generational reality in education, work, and retirement. Previously, life was conveniently divided into three neat compartments or "boxes" in which one activity predominated to the virtual exclusion of all others. From the age of birth to twenty-one, a person would be involved in education and learning; from twenty-two to sixty-five, in work; and from sixty-five on, in retirement or leisure. This model no longer holds. Retirement is now a new beginning rather than just an end. In this new view of retirement, a retiree can take the time to actively pursue new goals.

More so than any other group, the high net worth plan their retirement as thoroughly as the other areas of their life. They spend four or five years prior to full retirement planning how they will use the early and later retirement years. In making an action plan the high net worth will consider their interests, health, and the timing of family events, but the single defining factor that determines the couple's happiness and productivity in their sunset years is independence.

The high net worth have prepared themselves beforehand to fill their days with meaningful and varied activities that do not depend upon anyone else. The fact of the matter is that no one actually *practices* retirement until they either voluntarily or involuntarily plunge into it. The high-net-worth couple has already rehearsed and tried out different possible patterns (hobbies, community service, professional associations, charity work, education, youth development activities, volunteerism, etc.) that will take them into the last third of their life. Mature people are content to be by themselves and when they want to make new connections they find it easier than younger people. Retired people are more resilient, less self-conscious, and have more self-esteem than teenagers and young adults. Add in financial security and the high net worth can be downright flexible and adventurous.

The high income–low net worth in active retirement display a different mode. They scrimp and save in order to make ends meet, since they have not achieved the large investments and financial independence that will take them satisfactorily into their later retirement years.

The general tendency in American business is to retire no earlier than age sixty-two in order to take advantage of Social Security benefits. Many wait until sixty-five, and nearly all private and public businesses and institutions have an unwritten rule about mandatory retirement at seventy. Another consideration is that Individual Retirement Accounts (IRAs) and 401(k) funds by law cannot be withdrawn until a person turns fifty-nine and a half years old without paying a tax (usually at a higher rate due to higher income levels) and a hefty 10 percent penalty (unless the withdrawal meets the federal government's meaning of an "emergency").

Even with more choices today than in the past, the corporate high net worth still generally plan to leave between sixty-five and seventy, but many might remain on a part-time or consulting basis. There are examples such as Hunt-Wesson Foods and Rockwell International, where employees who left their full-time jobs at their companies have been hired by an outsourcing organization and returned to their former company on a contract basis as an external consultant. The corporate high net worth also might start a consulting practice, buy or start a business, or take the opportunity to change careers.

The entrepreneurial high net worth pretty much act the same as the corporate high-net-worth employee with one important exception—they understand the needs and problems of the small business owner. They might help out a friend who has a business on a part-time basis. If their children have a business, the parent might work on a part-time basis or consult.

Since a majority of the high net worth are in control of their own business or are professionals, such as physicians, lawyers, or accountants, they can plan to work full-time until age sixty-eight or seventy. A few remain involved in their business full-time well into their seventies and eighties with a sprinkling into their nineties. In 1999, according to the U.S. Bureau of Labor Statistics, 3.7 percent of people aged ninety or above were still in the American workforce. Some people of advanced age see retirement as a waste of their labor and talent. They share a high expectation of life and want meaningful and fulfilling experiences until the end. A structured work environment can play a role in prolonging their longevity and preserving their desire to feel needed and connected to the outside world.

Although working into their nineties is attractive to some, most of the high-net-worth entrepreneurs nonetheless plan on a gradual lightening of the workload. If they sell their company, they might stay on for a time as a consultant. If they keep the enterprise in the family, they work reduced hours. Many of the entrepreneurial high net worth will have even more money when they finally sell their business. A lucky few, who did not start out with the idea of becoming a high-net-worth household through real estate or the stock market, may become instant millionaires with the sale. Contrary to what most people might think, few businesses are actually passed on to children, who usually have established themselves in their own concern or profession.

In any case, the high net worth, whether entrepreneurial or corporate, are not ready to quit the workforce until their mortgage is paid up. On average, American households traditionally expend between 15 and 40 percent of the discretionary income each month to pay off their home. Once the mortgage is out of the way they have more discretionary income at their disposal to invest. Most retired high-net-worth couples tend to stay in the same house they have occupied for the past twenty years. Some couples may purchase mobile homes and extensively tour the country. In other cases, the couples may move to be closer to their family, move to a less expensive area of the country, or move to an area that interests them.

Sam B., a CPA who owned his own accounting practice, decided to sell his business at age sixty-five and move from the upper Midwest to the West Coast. He wasn't sure, however, which part of the West he and his wife, Mae, would like best. After selling their house, the couple leased a time-share condominium during the spring in a high-rise on Coronado Island, outside of San Diego, California. That summer, Sam and Mae took up residency in Palm Springs, California. During the fall and winter months, they explored Phoenix and Tucson.

Sam and Mae both realized that, while all of the areas offered ample opportunities to golf (their major form of recreation together), the moderate mean temperature in San Diego allowed the couple to do a lot more activities outdoors year-round.

Sam and Mae used the proceeds from the sale of their home to put a down payment on a condominium on Coronado Island. This became their home for more than fourteen years until Sam's death. Mae then sold the property for a handsome profit, returned to the upper Midwest to be closer to her family, and took up residency in an upscale retirement villa.

Albert L., a university professor of European history, left his tenured position at the age of sixty-five and decided to move to England. After selling their house in the tony Pacific Palisades area of Los Angeles, Albert and his wife, Pat, leased a residence from the Anglican Church outside London and used the apartment as their home base while they traveled extensively throughout Europe.

Occasionally, they would come back to the States to visit family. This continued for more than fifteen years. It was not until his mid-eighties that Albert began to slow down physically. Relinquishing the apartment lease in England and moving back to the U.S., Albert and Pat took up residency in a town house in the San Francisco Bay area to be closer to their four children.

The challenge of keeping up with the rapid changes in the business world has meant that a new commitment to lifelong learning has permeated American society. Enrollment for college students age sixty-five and older grew 27 percent from 1991 to 1995. More than 81,000 retirees are currently part- or full-time students. According to the U.S. Department of Education, there are another 356,000 students in the fifty to sixty-four age group. For retirees, traveling and learning through Elderhostel and Interhostel programs has become an extremely popular activity, one that is intellectually stimulating as well as physically venturesome.

Elderhostel programs are inexpensive, short-term (usually one week or more in length) academic courses for adults over sixty at colleges and universities around the country. Exploding in popularity, they currently attract 350,000 participants per year.

The Interhostel program is an opportunity to travel and study abroad at foreign institutions of higher learning. Courses are designed for people over fifty and last about two weeks. Interhostels offer field trips, excursions, lectures, and seminars led by American and foreign instructors, as well as outside experts. Again, participants usually stay at university accommodations around the world.

Another new trend has also captured the fancy of

aging alumni and retired college faculty. In recent years, approximately one hundred active adult communities (retirement communities) have been built near universities around the country. When one thinks of a retirement colony, the image is that of constant sunshine, golf dates, and outdoor barbecues. Many of these modern communities defy this stereotype by being situated in the northeast or Midwest with drizzly falls and stormy winter settings. What is more, in-line skating and weight training are as popular as golf for this new generation of retirees. Selling intellectual stimulation and interaction with college students, these campus retirement communities tap into retirees' nostalgia for a simpler time, the "halls of ivy" of the 1930s and 1940s. Going further than the Elderhostel programs, this type of residential community allows continuous contact with students as well as immersion in campus life. These living arrangements are a convenient target for alumni fund-raisers, because they bind high-net-worth retirees closer to their alma maters, resulting in more and larger financial gifts.

The implications of the elderly's desire for lifelong learning have not been lost on school administrators. The board of trustees at Pennsylvania State University approved in 1998 the development of a 160-acre planned community on university and privately owned land for people fifty-five years and older. As another example, Lasell College in Newton, Massachusetts, is taking on-campus retirement to a new level. An academic dean has been appointed by the college to head a division for the campus retirement community. This new "residential retirement" division will handle classes, field trips, volunteer work, and mentoring for this special category of lifelong learners. It is hoped the interaction of generations will reinvigorate the retired and link retirees and students.

In addition to on-campus living arrangements, many universities are also recognizing the profit potential of the group travel business for enticing prosperous alumni and guests. Competitive standard packages are offered as well as expensive educational versions called "affinity tours."

A new trend is also asserting itself in the late 1990s: urban gentrification. The ranks of retirees returning to urban centers from the suburbs are growing in some large cities. Anecdotal evidence suggests that hotels are being converted into assisted-living communities and the demand for rentals for the elderly is increasing in places such as Manhattan. Increasingly, grandparents want to be close to their kids and grandchildren.

Art Linkletter, a former TV talk show host, once remarked that the four stages of life were infancy, childhood, adolescence, and obsolescence. That last phase represents a troublesome false perception. Retirement should be viewed as a time for people to develop themselves more fully. It should not be hectic and overstressed, but it should not be boring either.

RETIREMENT IN THE NEW MILLENNIUM

Generally during the first decade of retirement, the average high-net-worth household lives on less than the total amount of interest and income generated by all of their combined investments, pensions, 401(k) plans, and

Social Security benefits. In many cases, they have more money at their disposal each month through these sources than what the family had received in gross income before retirement. It is not out of the ordinary for the high-net-worth couple to reinvest this excess income. Assuming a 10 percent rate of return on $1 million, the average millionaire lives on 7 percent of their wealth, or about $70,000 per year. This leaves more than $30,000 to be reinvested for later retirement. Social Security may add another $10,000-$25,000 per year to the total. Used to living a careful, disciplined lifestyle, these families continue the same pattern of spending.

Figuring they might live a long time in retirement, perhaps twenty-five to thirty years, the high-net-worth couple will rarely spend enough to consume their net worth in their lifetimes. This is typical of $1 million-net-worth families. If they only touch the money earned on interest, without touching the principal, the money will last indefinitely. With money left over each year from interest, the retirees' principal will continue to grow. Many high-net-worth households have enough to leave a considerable amount to charities, foundations, non-profit organizations, and educational institutions of their choosing.

There is also the matter of giving gifts. Federal law allows up to $10,000 to be given away each year per person without the benefactor having to pay gift or estate taxes. Usually, the retired high-net-worth couple gives an annual gift to each grandchild.

On August 5, 1997, President Clinton signed into law the Taxpayer Relief Act, the most significant tax legislation in more than a decade. It embodied more than eight hundred amendments to the Internal Revenue Code, one of which was the "unified credit against estate and gift tax." Two of the more important provisions relating to gifts include: 1) Beginning in 1999, the $10,000-per-person annual exclusion for gifts will be indexed for inflation and rounded to the next lowest multiple of $1,000; and, more importantly, 2) starting in 1998 and extending through 2006, the credit increases annually in a series of steps: In 1999 the $650,000 exemption ($1.3 million for a married couple) will increase to $675,000 ($1.35 million for a married couple) for the years 2000 and 2001; the exemption then increases to $700,000 ($1.4 million for a couple) for the years 2002 and 2003, $850,000 ($1.7 million for a couple) in the year 2004, $950,000 ($1.9 million for a couple) in the year 2005 to a maximum of $1 million ($2 million for a couple) in the year 2006.

Should a high-net-worth family be interested in bequeathing the bulk of their estate to their children, or other close family members, many households bring down the net worth to the level where federal income tax is not an issue. A high-net-worth parent or grandparent can use the $10,000 annual gift to help transfer additional assets out of an estate prior to their death. Also, the high-net-worth family has a propensity to use a life insurance policy to pay off or reimburse estate taxes due the federal or state government.

The high net worth purchase private hospitalization plans unless their former employer has a provision allowing them to remain on the company's group health plan. They may also take advantage of Medicare. The high net worth as a group have the best health-care coverage, since they can tap into their private reserve of cash, if need be, to get choice care. The largest economic group in the American population, the low net worth, does not have the same flexibility. Without a vast change in national health care, it will not be a pleasant future for low-net-worth families. They may one day need to take financial assistance from their immediate family, or even move in with a grown child in order to live out their elderly years.

If they are eligible, the high net worth also file for their Social Security benefits. They accept what is due them and are not too proud to turn it down. The same cannot be said for the high income–low net worth. Because of lingering image and status considerations, they may decline Social Security, Medicare, disability, or unemployment benefits. Should the Social Security system fail thirty years from now, millions of Americans will be adversely affected. Remember that Social Security accounts for 70 percent or more of the gross income for families in the bottom 25 percent in savings in this country.

SIGNPOSTS

RETIREMENT

A majority of Americans will have no choice but to work full- or part-time to get by financially during retirement.

I. **TRADITIONALLY, SOCIAL SECURITY IS SUPPOSED TO ACCOUNT FOR 20 PERCENT OF A WORKER'S TOTAL RETIREMENT FUND. THE REST IS SUPPOSED TO BE MADE UP OF A WORKER'S OWN INVESTMENTS, A POSSIBLE PENSION, A 401(K), AND OTHER COMPANY-SPONSORED SAVINGS. FOR MILLIONS OF AMERICANS, SOCIAL SECURITY PROVIDES 70 PERCENT OR MORE OF THEIR RETIREMENT MONEY.**

a. Unless reforms are enacted, Social Security will only be able to pay out 75 percent of benefits by the year 2032.

b. To aid the plight of Social Security, Congress has moved the age at which a person begins receiving full benefits from sixty-five to sixty-six for those born in and after 1943, and to sixty-seven for those born in and after 1960.

c. Increased immigration in the years ahead will bring more funds into the Social Security system but will not be nearly enough to bail it out.

d. Currently, there is debate in Congress whether to raise the age for full benefits to seventy, to privatize or semi-privatize some or all of the Social Security funds, or to increase taxation to boost the Social Security coffers.

e. Until Social Security is reformed, people may have to rely on Social Security payments for less of their retirement income.

2. IN THE YEAR 2005 IT IS ESTIMATED THAT 5 PERCENT OF THE AMERICAN POPULATION WILL HAVE A NET WORTH OF $1 MILLION OR GREATER, UP FROM TODAY'S 4.1 PERCENT.

a. Another 15 percent will have investments, pensions, 401(k) plans, and Social Security to take them at least fifteen years into retirement.

b. In order for the other 80 percent of the population to raise their net worth to have enough money for retirement, they will have to change their spending and investing habits.

3. HIGH-NET-WORTH HOUSEHOLDS CAN RETIRE EARLY WITHOUT A FINANCIAL PROBLEM.

a. Early retirement for people in their fifties and sixties often means second careers or consulting.

b. Company-defined benefit plans (pensions) can be tricky and need to be carefully examined to find out when to retire in order to receive the best benefits. Most of the high net worth take their pension in a lump sum rather than in monthly payments because they expect to earn greater returns through direct investment.

4. ACTIVE RETIREMENT FOR THE HIGH NET WORTH WILL BE AN EXCITING TIME.

a. After selling their businesses, many entrepreneurs will find themselves instant millionaires.

b. High-net-worth people often spend their early retirement years in part-time work, hobbies, volunteering, or consulting. A few remain in full-time work but either change careers, consult, or buy or start a business.

c. Most people in the high-net-worth category do not quit the workforce for good until the mortgage is paid up.

d. Often, the high net worth find they have more money coming in yearly from investments ($60,000–$100,000) than they ever earned when they were working full-time.

5. LATE RETIREMENT (EIGHTY-ONE YEARS OF AGE AND UP)

a. The high-net-worth household will begin to expend their principal.

b. Current federal law allows each person to give away up to $10,000 per year without incurring a tax liability.

c. In 1999, an individual can leave an estate worth $650,000 and a couple can bequeath up to $1.3 million tax-free. This goes up in stages until the year 2006, when the sum will be $1 million and $2 million, respectively.

d. The $10,000 tax-free gift each year can be used to

pare an estate to the appropriate level.

e. Couples can also ensure their estate will remain intact through a living trust.

f. The high net worth often use a life insurance policy to pay federal and state estate taxes.

6. PLANNING FOR RETIREMENT.

a. High-net-worth households frequently spend four or five years prior to full retirement planning how they will use the early retirement years.

b. In making an action plan, they consider their interests, health issues, and the timing of family events.

c. Since people are taking better care of themselves, families should plan for at least twenty-five years for retirement—the last third of their lives.

d. High-net-worth retirees are generally independent and have high self-esteem.

e. They either live in their paid-up home, or move to another part of the country.

f. The high net worth purchase private hospital plans, if they are not covered by their former company's group health plan.

g. They file for Social Security benefits at the appropriate time.

10

PAY THE PRICE

OVER THE LAST FIFTY YEARS, THE UNITED STATES has built the strongest economy in the world. At the same time, Americans rank well below the world average in savings. One of the most disturbing trends economists have tracked has been the steady erosion of the savings rate. Today's Americans have accumulated less for retirement than previous generations.

For example, in 1997 Americans saved less than 2.1 percent of their income, less than *one-quarter* the savings rate (9 percent) in 1975. In 1998, after approximately $100 billion in extra spending by American consumers, the personal savings rate fell to .5 percent. (Granted, the government has a curious definition of savings that does not consider the value of pensions, 401(k) accounts or IRAs that now account for a greater portion of a family's net worth than ever before.)

Despite the dismal savings rate, it seems Americans are feeling wealthier. While workers are stepping up their contributions to their company-sponsored 401(k) plans, they are at the same time taking money out of their individual stock and mutual fund accounts and spending nearly all of their discretionary take-home pay.

Financial experts estimate 45 percent of American workers have money troubles and 15 percent have serious financial problems. Although the economy is having the best bout of growth since World War II and the United States remains remarkably unscathed so far by financial upheavals in Asia, consumer installment credit reached a cumulative $1.25 trillion in 1998. In 1999 it climbed to $1.34 trillion, a record high. On average, each American family is in consumer debt, excluding mortgages, by a sum approximating $13,400, up from $12,500 in 1998.

For most families, the home happens to be the single largest investment they have. When equity builds slowly over time people feel they are becoming more prosperous, but when home prices escalate rapidly families experience the "wealth effect." High income–low net worth consumers are likely to spend more for goods and services. They will sell their existing homes to buy larger, more expensive residences; to remodel their existing home; to consolidate and pay down consumer debt; to buy expensive commodities such as cars, boats, or small aircraft; to pay for college tuition; or to start a new business.

According to mortgage companies, some families have increased their consumer debt during the last few years of prosperity to untenably high levels of $40,000–$100,000. Without discipline, many of these families will begin to charge on their many credit cards again, while continuing to pay off their first mortgage and an equity loan that costs several hundred dollars a month. As the cycle of increased debt is repeated, a sizeable number of them will inevitably go bankrupt.

The same behavior is seen with high income–low net worth households who own individual stock or have mutual fund portfolios. In prosperous times when a profit has been made, these investors are inclined to cash out to help fund the purchase of expensive homes or other goods.

Millions of workers today are dependent on 401(k) plans or IRAs to provide for their retirement. Right now, these plans are growing at a record pace. But employers worry that if the stock market turns downward, they will be blamed for the lower returns and so they are bracing themselves for litigation. If the market drops, millions of workers will probably pull their money out of the stock market, while the high-net-worth group will be savvy enough to take advantage of the crisis by buying up stocks at bargain-basement prices.

Today, there are 34 million people sixty-five years of age and older, representing approximately 12 percent of the nation's population. This group will double to nearly 70 million by the year 2020, about 20 percent of the projected population. And very few of these people have saved for a world where they might live twenty-five to thirty years after retiring.

The Urban Institute conducted a study predicting that baby boomers will reach retirement age with less than half the real net worth their parents, the so-called traditionalists, had at a similar age. It is estimated that boomers will begin retiring in the year 2011 with an average net worth of $143,000, compared with the average of $293,000 their parents enjoy today.

Emboldened by today's prosperity, Americans have a unique opportunity to ensure themselves a rosy economic future. In order to avert a nationwide financial crisis, we should all look to the example of the high-net-worth households and learn to live below our means, invest often and consistently, and protect our investments. It is psychologically comforting to know most millionaires made their money on their own—80 percent are first-generation millionaires—and nearly anyone today can do it in the same manner.

One technique people use is to print their goal on a card with a realistic date of when they expect to achieve it. Then they look at that card each day in a calm, relaxed, cheerful manner. Next, they set up a "millionaire tax," taking from 10–50 percent off the top of their paycheck to invest. Then they pay off their bills with the remaining money. In other words, the idea is to pay yourself first, then your fixed expenses, followed by discretionary expenditures.

This plan will work wonders. People are highly adaptive and new traits can be acquired at any age and any stage of life. Although the first few months will be difficult, the process will soon become second nature, and your lifestyle will adjust. Once the new pattern is formed it will be difficult to break.

In the first month or two, you might find yourself off your target of saving a specified amount. Do not fret. Just start over again. Determine that in the next month you will pay yourself first, pay the bills next, and lower the household's discretionary expenses. It might take a little time to get on track and establish this as an ingrained practice. Remember not to let petty annoyances or distractions throw you off target. Keep your financial goals in front of you. Soon, the new behavior of saving and investing will take hold and you will forget how your life could have been any different. In discussions with households that have gotten used to living a simpler lifestyle, it becomes clear that there is very little a family must spend money on other than food, clothing, shelter, transportation, and taxes.

If your investments—in your 401(k), other company-sponsored benefit plans, your own investment portfolio of stocks, IRAs, mutual funds, and possibly real estate—can return at least 8 percent or more, and should the bull market of the 1990s continue, you and your family will be on the road to riches. (Refer to Appendix V.)

All through this book I have tried to describe what I have learned from the high-net-worth people I have known and worked with during my life. The old saying that the rich are different from you and me is *true*, and I have done my best to show just how different they are. But if you remember only one thing from this book, know that you can cross over and become one of them if you are willing to adopt the practices that have worked so successfully in the past. In just a single generation, you can transform your family into a high-net-worth family, no matter how humble your beginnings or how lowly your current job. You don't have to make a lot of money to become wealthy, and I believe that making a lot of money can sometimes become a hindrance to developing a high net worth.

The path that I have outlined is an old-fashioned one. It requires you to develop an independent mind that shuts out the constant societal refrain that getting and spending is the way to happiness. It requires the postponement of short-term pleasure in order to accomplish long-term goals. It requires self-discipline and planning ahead. Putting aside the financial benefits, aren't these qualities that are worth developing for their own sake? Our parents and grandparents certainly thought so.

The time has never been better for putting this plan into action. I hope you start today.

APPENDIX I

THE 401(K)

THE VAST MAJORITY OF 401(K)S ARE SALARY-reduction plans that permit an investor to make regular pretax contributions through convenient payroll deductions. Under this type of arrangement, the 401(k) pretax contributions are deducted from the current-year pay for federal and state (with the exception of Pennsylvania) income tax purposes.

Many 401(k) plans provide for matching contributions by the employer. In fact, nearly all large companies match some portion of each employee's pretax contributions, and one out of every four matches dollar for dollar, up to specified levels. Matching contributions are a powerful incentive for employees at all income levels to participate in a 401(k) to the maximum extent possible.

A few examples will show how powerful this defined contribution plan can be.

EXAMPLE 1

You are working for an employer who will contribute up to $3,000 to your account. You want to take advantage of what the company will put in for you, but you decide not to contribute at all from your income. You would rather spend your income on your lifestyle. This continues into the future.

$3,000 PUT ASIDE PER YEAR BY EMPLOYER ALONE	VALUE AT 10% RETURN
Years 1–5	$18,315
Years 6–10	$47,812
Years 11–15	$95,317
Years 16–20	$171,825
Years 21–25	$295,041
Years 26–30	$493,482

EXAMPLE 2

You decide to put aside $6,000 per year and your employer will match your contributions up to 50 percent ($3,000). The total amount put aside will be $6,000 + $3,000 = $9,000 per year.

$9,000 PUT ASIDE PER YEAR	VALUE AT 10% RETURN
Years 1–5	$54,945
Years 6–10	$143,436
Years 11–15	$285,952
Years 16–20	$515,475
Years 21–25	$885,123
Years 26–30	$1,480,440

EXAMPLE 3

You take full advantage of the maximum allowable in your 401(k) account—$9,500—and your employer will put in the $3,000 maximum. The total put aside per year will be $9,500 + $3,000 = $12,500.

$9,000 PUT ASIDE PER YEAR	VALUE AT 10% RETURN
Years 1–5	$76,313
Years 6–10	$199,217
Years 11–15	$397,156
Years 16–20	$715,937
Years 21–25	$1,229,338
Years 26–30	$2,056,175

THIRTY-YEAR SUMMARY

EMPLOYER ALONE PUTTING ASIDE $3,000 PER YEAR	=	$493,482
EMPLOYEE AND EMPLOYER COMBINED, $9,000 PER YEAR	=	$1,480,440
EMPLOYEE AND EMPLOYER COMBINED, $12,500 PER YEAR	=	$2,056,175

The 401(k) is an easy, convenient, and painless way to acquire $1 million net worth. Most American households have two full-time incomes. Should both partners put away money in a 401(k) account with their employers, it is easily possible that combined they will have $1 million at the end of their working life.

In deciding whether to put aside the maximum

allowable in a 401(k) account, an investor is making a million-dollar decision. Do you want to spend your wealth today, or invest it in order to ensure a $1 million net worth at retirement?

401(K) WORKSHEET

Maximum pretax contribution to your 401(k)

$_____

+

Employer Contribution

$_____

=

Total Contribution

$_____

EMPLOYER AND EMPLOYEE 401(K) CONTRIBUTIONS

HOW LONG IT WILL TAKE	VALUE AT 10% RETURN
Years 1–5	$_____
Years 6–10	$_____
Years 11–15	$_____
Years 16–20	$_____
Years 21–25	$_____
Years 26–30	$_____

APPENDIX II

HOUSING

FOR THE AVERAGE AMERICAN HOUSEHOLD, THE cost of buying and paying for a house is their greatest single expenditure. With a fixed mortgage rate over thirty years, a family will be paying a smaller proportion of their income over time as their pay progressively increases. The savings here can be used as discretionary income for investment purposes. This fact is lost, however, on a large portion of the population who insist on buying increasingly larger and more expensive houses during their work history.

This section will demonstrate how much money can be saved—and invested—if you resist that temptation.

EXAMPLE I

Let's say a family bought a house in 1978 for $99,995. By making monthly payments of $644 for twenty years, they have paid down the original $79,995 mortgage to $60,000. In 1999, they can sell the home for $325,000. If they sell the house and assume it will cost 8 percent for closing costs, then 8 percent of $325,000 = $26,000.

$325,000	MARKET VALUE OF HOUSE
− $26,000	CLOSING COST ON THE HOUSE'S SALE
$299,000	GROSS PROFIT

$299,000	GROSS PROFIT
− $60,000	EXISTING MORTGAGE
$239,000	NET PROFIT FROM SALE

EXAMPLE 2

That same family decides to purchase a $500,000 home in a newly completed development. They take the proceeds from the previous sale and apply all of it to the new mortgage.

$500,000	COST OF NEW HOME
− $239,000	DOWN PAYMENT
$261,000	COST OF NEW MORTGAGE

At a 9 percent interest rate, the family's $261,000 mortgage will cost $2,100 per month for 360 months (thirty years). The difference between $2,100 and the $644 per-month payment on their old home is $1,456 per month. If the $1,456 per month were invested instead, this is what it would look like:

HOW LONG IT WILL TAKE	VALUE AT 10% RETURN
5 Years	$112,748
10 Years	$298,254
15 Years	$403,468
20 Years	$1,105,641
25 Years	$1,931,869
30 Years	$3,291,270

SUMMARY

1. On a house bought twenty years ago for $99,995 and sold for $325,000, the net profit is $299,000. Subtracting what is still owed on the house leaves $261,000. This is a sound investment. If the family were to remain in the house for another ten years, the house would be paid for and the couple could retire, living in the residence mortgage free.

2. If the house were sold for $325,000, and the family used the profit to purchase a $500,000 house, it will cost $2,100 a month in mortgage payments. This is almost 3.5 times more than the mortgage payments on the original $99,995 house.

3. Rather than purchase a $500,000 house, the family invests the difference between $2,100 and $644 per month (the mortgage on the $99,995 house). This gives them $1,456 per month with which to work. At 10% interest, in twenty years they would have a net worth of $1 million; in twenty-five years they would have nearly $2 million; and in thirty years the family would have in excess of $3.2 million.

4. Families with more than $100,000 in combined incomes are buying even more expensive homes— $750,000 and up. The investment of the difference between a high mortgage and the $644 per month example would have an even greater effect. A family could attain millionaire status even faster.

5. A larger home means higher property taxes, utilities, and maintenance. If this money were invested rather than put into a more expensive residence, the family would be able to increase its net worth faster.

In deciding whether to buy a more expensive home, a family is making a million-dollar decision whether to spend and live in one's wealth or to invest that wealth and have it in a portfolio for retirement.

IF YOU WERE TO BUY A NEW HOME WORKSHEET

Price of new home

$ _____

Less market value of current home

$ _____   = $ _____

Less 8 percent closing costs on current home

$ _____   = $ _____

Less current home's mortgage to date

$ _____   = $ _____

New home mortgage

$ _____

SECTION 2

New home mortgage payment at 9 percent for thirty years

$ _____

Less current home's mortgage payment

$ _____   = $ _____

Monthly investment

$ _____

SECTION 3

AMOUNT OF TIME
FOR INVESTING   VALUE AT 10% RETURN

AMOUNT OF TIME FOR INVESTING	VALUE AT 10% RETURN
5 Years	$ _____
10 Years	$ _____
15 Years	$ _____
20 Years	$ _____
25 Years	$ _____
30 Years	$ _____

APPENDIX III

AUTOMOBILES

FOR MOST HOUSEHOLDS, THE COST AND EXPense of owning a new car is the second largest expenditure next to their house. Most American families have more than one car and a large number of high-income families are making payments on more than one new car at a time. The expense of buying a new automobile every five years is quite high. This takes into account not only the initial cost and interest paid over the life of the loan, but also the car's depreciation of about 50 percent in the first three years of ownership.

The following examples will demonstrate the cost of new car ownership. With expensive luxury autos, the expense of owning such a car over a person's working life can be equivalent to the amount spent on an average house.

EXAMPLE I

A consumer decides to purchase an average American four-door sedan. For convenience in working out the calculations, let us consider a car that initially costs $20,000.

Initial car cost		$20,000
Sales tax	+	$1,050
License & registration fee	+	$438
	=	$21,988
	–	$5,000 down payment
Finance amount		$16,988

Payment = $353 per month; five years at 9 percent interest

Payment ($353)x 60 months	=	$21,180
Add down payment	+	$ 5,000
True cost	=	$26,180

EXAMPLE 2

In the second example, let us compare purchasing a $20,000 car every five years versus holding the original car (paid for after five years) for an additional twenty years and investing the money instead at a 10 percent return.

	NEW CAR EVERY 5 YEARS	10% RETURN ON INVESTMENT
Years 1–5	$26,180	0
Years 6–10	$26,180	$27,335
Years 11–15	$26,180	$72,310
Years 16–20	$26,180	$146,308
Years 21–25	$26,180	$268,057
Total	– $130,900	

$130,900	Paid to finance company
+ $268,057	Lost opportunity
$398,957	Difference

EXAMPLE 3

In the third example, let us compare leasing a $60,000 automobile for five years and then leasing every five years thereafter versus investing the money at 10 percent interest.

Leasing a $60,000 car

Initial car cost		$60,000
Sales tax	+	$4,650
License & registration fee	+	$1,238
Total cost	=	$65,888

Loan payment = $820 per month

$820/month x 60 months = $49,200

Residual value = $26,081 after five years

	LEASE CAR EVERY 5 YEARS	10% RETURN ON INVESTMENT
Years 1–5	$49,200	0
Years 6–10	$49,200	$63,498
Years 11–15	$49,200	$167,972
Years 16–20	$49,200	$339,865
Years 21–25	$49,200	$622,682
Total	–$246,000	

Return on Investment		$622,682
Residual Value	–	$26,081
Lost opportunity		$596,601
Paid to lease company	+	$246,000
Difference		$842,601

EXAMPLE 4

In the fourth example, let us say we buy a $60,000 car through third-party financing, hold the car for twenty more years, and invest the money instead at a 10 percent return.

Payment: $1,465 per month

	BUY CAR WITH FINANCING	10% RETURN ON INVESTMENT
Years 1–5	$87,900	0
Years 6–10	$0	$113,445
Years 11–15	$0	$300,097
Years 16–20	$0	$607,199
Years 21–25	$0	$1,112,475

EXAMPLE 5

In this example, let us compare buying a $60,000 luxury car for cash and holding it for twenty-five years versus investing our savings ($1,465 per month) at a 10 percent return.

	BUY CAR WITH CASH	10% RETURN ON INVESTMENT
Years 1–5	$68,888	$113,445
Years 6–10	$0	$300,097
Years 11–15	$0	$607,199
Years 16–20	$0	$1,112,475
Years 21–25	$0	$1,943,810

SUMMARY

LEASING EVERY FIVE YEARS FOR TWENTY YEARS	**– $246,000**
LEASE FOR FIVE YEARS AND RETAIN CAR TWENTY YEARS MORE	**+ $596,601**
BUY ONCE WITH THIRD PARTY FINANCING	**+ $1,112,475**
BUY ONCE AND PAY CASH	**+ $1,943,810**

Most people have not investigated how the cost of an automobile figures over the course of their working life. This expense is compounded by families owning more than one car and buying vehicles for their children once they receive a driver's license.

Paying cash for an automobile and repaying yourself is the way to a $1 million retirement. The key is to figure out the monthly payment to yourself based on current bank lending terms. Then continue to make this monthly payment to your investments for twenty years rather than buy a new car every five years. The choice is yours. In purchasing a new car every five years, you are making a million-dollar decision whether to spend and drive your wealth or to invest it and have a $1 million portfolio when you retire.

AUTOMOBILE WORKSHEET

Price of new car	$	_____
State sales tax	+ $	_____
License & registration fee	+ $	_____
Total car cost	= $	_____
Down payment	− $	_____
Actual car cost	= $	_____
Car payment at 9% interest for 60 months	$	_____

If you were to invest the money instead, and drive either a new car that you bought with cash or a previously owned vehicle, this is what you would find:

AMOUNT OF TIME FOR INVESTING	VALUE AT 10% RETURN
5 Years	$ _____
10 Years	$ _____
15 Years	$ _____
20 Years	$ _____
25 Years	$ _____
30 Years	$ _____

APPENDIX IV

INDIVIDUAL RETIREMENT ACCOUNT (IRA)

THE INDIVIDUAL RETIREMENT ACCOUNT (IRA) is a self-funded retirement plan allowing employed individuals to contribute up to $2,000 per year toward their retirement. If a single taxpayer earns less than $25,000 per year, they can deduct the IRA contribution from their federal income tax. If a married taxpayer filing jointly earns less than $40,000 per year, regardless of whether either spouse is an active participant in a qualified retirement plan, they can do the same.

The IRA is an important tool for wealth creation, and an investor should put the $2,000 maximum in the account each year, preferably in January, in order to receive the interest on that amount for the entire year.

$2,000 PUT ASIDE EACH YEAR	VALUE AT 10% RETURN
Years 1–5	$12,210
Years 6–10	$31,581
Years 11–15	$63,071
Years 16–20	$113,788
Years 21–25	$195,471
Years 26–30	$327,018
Years 31–35	$538,877
Years 36–40	$880,078

THIRTY-FIVE YEAR SUMMARY

INVESTOR SETTING ASIDE $2,000 PER YEAR	=	$538,877

MARRIED COUPLE BOTH SETTING ASIDE $2,000 PER YEAR	=	$1,077,754

The IRA is another easy, painless way to acquire $1 million net worth. Most American households have two full-time incomes. Should both partners put $2,000 each year in an IRA account, it is very possible that they will have $1 million combined at the end of their working life.

In deciding whether to put aside $2,000 per year in an IRA account, you are making a million-dollar decision. Do you want to spend your wealth today or invest it in order to ensure a net worth of $1 million at your retirement?

IRA WORKSHEET

Contribution to your IRA $ _____

Contribution to your
spouse's IRA   + $ _____

Total contribution $ _____

HOW LONG IT WILL TAKE YOUR IRA	**VALUE AT 10% RETURN**
Years 1–5	$ _____
Years 6–10	$ _____
Years 11–15	$ _____
Years 16–20	$ _____
Years 21–25	$ _____
Years 26–30	$ _____
Years 31–35	$ _____
Years 36–40	$ _____

HOW LONG IT WILL TAKE YOUR SPOUSE'S IRA	**VALUE AT 10% RETURN**
Years 1–5	$ _____
Years 6–10	$ _____
Years 11–15	$ _____
Years 16–20	$ _____
Years 21–25	$ _____
Years 26–30	$ _____
Years 31–35	$ _____
Years 36–40	$ _____

Total of your contribution $ _____

Total of your spouse's
contribution   + $ _____

IRA Grand Total   = $ _____

APPENDIX V

SUMMARY

THE FOLLOWING ARE THE HYPOTHETICAL OPTImal earnings one can generate over a thirty-year period, based upon the figures used in the worksheets in the preceding appendices.

APPENDIX I: 401(K)
$2,056,175

APPENDIX II: HOUSE
$3,291,270

APPENDIX III: AUTOMOBILE
$1,943,810

APPENDIX IV: INDIVIDUAL RETIREMENT ACCOUNT
$1,077,754

YOUR FINANCIAL GOALS

$ _____ 401(k)

$ _____ House

$ _____ Automobile

$ _____ Individual Retirement Account

You are on your way. Any of the four steps above, either alone or in combination, can put you well on the road to your goal of $1 million at retirement.

READER RESPONSE

WE WOULD BE INTERESTED TO GATHER THE views of our readers. You may have an interesting anecdote, idea, or suggestion for future editions of this book (or other books). In addition, should you be on your way to $1 million net worth or have already achieved it, we would also like to hear from you about your experiences.

My e-mail address is: **markalch@deltanet.com**
You can also look up our site on the Web at
www.markalch.com

You can also write to us at:
　Mark Alch & Associates
　c/o Update
　PMB 418
　4790 Irvine Boulevard, Suite 105
　Irvine, CA 92620-1998